SPACE AND ILLUSION IN
THE JAPANESE GARDEN

SPACE AND  ILLUSION

IN THE JAPANESE GARDEN

text by Teiji Itoh

photographs by Sosei Kuzunishi

translated and adapted from the Japanese by

Ralph Friedrich and Masajiro Shimamura

WEATHERHILL/TANKOSHA
New York, Tokyo & Kyoto

This book was originally published in Japanese in 1965 by Tankosha, Kyoto, under the title Shakkei to Tsuboniwa *(Borrowed Scenery and Courtyard Gardens).*

FIRST ENGLISH EDITION, 1973

Jointly published by John Weatherhill, Inc., of New York and Tokyo; and Tankosha, of Kyoto. Distributed by John Weatherhill, Inc., 149 Madison Avenue, New York, N.Y. 10016, with editorial offices at 7-6-13 Roppongi, Minato-ku, Tokyo. Copyright © 1965, 1973 by Tankosha; all rights reserved. Printed in Japan.

Library of Congress Cataloging in Publication Data: Itō, Teiji, 1922– / Space and illusion in the Japanese garden. / 1. Gardens, Japanese. / 2. Gardens—Japan. / I. Kuzunishi, Sōsei, illus. / II. Title. / SB458.I8713 / 712'.2 / 72-89445 / ISBN 0-8348-1512-5

TABLE OF CONTENTS

	List of Illustrations	7
	Foreword	11
1.	To Capture Alive	15
2.	To Command a Good View	18
3.	To Constitute a Shakkei Garden	29
4.	To Capture with Tree Trunks	33
5.	To Capture with a Woods	39
6.	To Capture with Posts and Eaves	45
7.	To Capture with the Sky	48
8.	To Capture with a Stone Lantern	54
9.	To Capture with a Window	57
10.	The Birth of the Courtyard Garden	59
11.	Hidden Retreats in the City	65
12.	Three Forms of the Courtyard Garden	70
13.	A Distillation of Culture	75
14.	Three Components of the Courtyard Garden	80
15.	The Essence of the Courtyard Garden	86
	Photographs	93
	Commentaries on the Photographs	213
	Appendix: Locations of Representative Gardens	227

LIST OF ILLUSTRATIONS

1. Courtyard garden, Yamato Bunkakan art museum, Nara   93
2. Detail of borrowed-landscape garden, Jiko-in, Yamato Koriyama, Nara Prefecture   94
3. Detail of tea garden, Shoka-do, Iwashimizu Hachiman Shrine, Kyoto   94
4. View of Upper Garden and borrowed scenery, Shugaku-in, Kyoto   95
5. Ritual water basin and accompanying stones, Shoka-do tea garden, Iwashimizu Hachiman Shrine, Kyoto   96
6. View of Mount Hiei from Shoden-ji temple garden, Kyoto   98
7. View of Lake Biwa from Tennenzue-tei, Otsu, Shiga Prefecture   99
8. View of Arashiyama from garden of Kitcho restaurant, Kyoto   100
9. Rin'un-tei, Shugaku-in, Kyoto   101
10. View from Upper Garden, Shugaku-in, Kyoto   102
11. View from Rin'un-tei, Shugaku-in, Kyoto   104
12. View across Pond of the Bathing Dragon, Upper Garden, Shugaku-in, Kyoto   105
13. View from north shore of pond, Upper Garden, Shugaku-in, Kyoto   106
14. Main gate, Middle Garden, Shugaku-in, Kyoto   108
15. Chinese-style bridge, Upper Garden, Shugaku-in, Kyoto   109
16. Path leading to Middle Garden, Shugaku-in, Kyoto   110
17. View of Entsu-ji temple garden, Kyoto   111
18. View of Mount Hiei from Entsu-ji garden, Kyoto   112
19. Shrubbery at front gate, Entsu-ji, Kyoto   114
20. Pond and garden paths, Murin-an, Kyoto   115
21. Murin-an garden, Kyoto   116
22. Detail of pond and shore, Murin-an garden, Kyoto   118

23. Murin-an garden, Kyoto 120

24. Brook and rocks, Shinshin-an garden, Kyoto 121

25. Island and stone pagoda, Shinshin-an garden, Kyoto 122

26. Cryptomeria grove, Shinshin-an garden, Kyoto 124

27. View of main gate, Nanzen-ji temple, from Shinshin-an garden, Kyoto 126

28. Detail of Joju-in garden, Kiyomizu-dera, Kyoto 127

29. Borrowed scenery, Joju-in garden, Kiyomizu-dera, Kyoto 128

30. Tenryu-ji temple, Kyoto 129

31. Rock arrangement and detail of pond, Tenryu-ji garden, Kyoto 130

32, 33. Borrowed scenery, Tenryu-ji garden, Kyoto 132

34. Approach to Jiko-in garden, Yamato Koriyama, Nara Prefecture 134

35, 36. Borrowed scenery, Jiko-in garden, Yamato Koriyama, Nara Prefecture 135

37. View of Great South Gate, Todai-ji temple, from Isui-en garden, Nara 137

38. Isui-en garden and borrowed scenery, Nara 138

39. Pond and steppingstones, Isui-en garden, Nara 140

40. Detail of courtyard garden, Kyoto Imperial Palace 141

41. Courtyard garden, Ninna-ji temple, Kyoto 142

42. Courtyard garden, Kamigamo Shrine, Kyoto 143

43. Courtyard garden, priests' quarters, Ginkaku-ji, Kyoto 144

44. Detail of garden, Ginkaku-ji, Kyoto 146

45, 46. Courtyard garden, meditation hall, Kennin-ji, Kyoto 147

47. Detail of courtyard garden, meditation hall, Kennin-ji, Kyoto 149

48, 49. Courtyard garden, Hossho-in, Ishiyama-dera, Otsu, Shiga Prefecture 150

50. Steppingstone paths in courtyard garden, Ryosoku-in, Kennin-ji, Kyoto 152

51. Stone-paved path in tea garden, Ura Senke, Kyoto 153

52. Tea-garden path, Ura Senke, Kyoto 154

53. Tea-garden path leading to waiting booth, Ura Senke, Kyoto 156

54. Approach to teahouse, Ura Senke, Kyoto 157

55. Ritual water basin and accompanying stones, Ura Senke, Kyoto 158

56. Detail of rear garden, Ura Senke, Kyoto 160

57. Detail of tea garden, Ura Senke, Kyoto 162

58. Detail of garden and surrounding veranda, Ura Senke, Kyoto 163

59. Detail of courtyard garden, Ura Senke, Kyoto 164

60. Approach to main entrance, Omote Senke, Kyoto ... *165*

61. Detail of main entrance, Omote Senke, Kyoto ... *166*

62. Window-gate in tea garden, Omote Senke, Kyoto ... *167*

63. Steppingstone arrangement in tea garden, Omote Senke, Kyoto ... *168*

64. Detail of tea garden, Omote Senke, Kyoto ... *169*

65. Steppingstone path in tea garden, Omote Senke, Kyoto ... *170*

66. Stone-paved walk and waiting bench, Kankyu-an, Mushanokoji Senke, Kyoto ... *171*

67. Detail of tea garden, Kankyu-an, Mushanokoji Senke, Kyoto ... *172*

68. Ritual water basin and accompanying stones, Yabunouchi school of tea, Kyoto ... *173*

69. Tea-garden path, Yabunouchi school of tea, Kyoto ... *174*

70. Detail of tea-garden path, Yabunouchi school of tea, Kyoto ... *175*

71. Under-eaves area and waiting bench, Hyo-tei restaurant, Kyoto ... *176*

72. Approach to teahouse, Hyo-tei restaurant, Kyoto ... *177*

73. Tea-garden pond, Hyo-tei restaurant, Kyoto ... *178*

74. Exterior of teahouse, Hyo-tei restaurant, Kyoto ... *179*

75. Approach to main entrance, Daimonjiya inn, Kyoto ... *180*

76. Courtyard garden adjacent to main entrance, Daimonjiya inn, Kyoto ... *181*

77. Guest-room courtyard garden in tea-garden style, Daimonjiya inn, Kyoto ... *182*

78. Guest-room courtyard garden in Zen style, Daimonjiya inn, Kyoto ... *183*

79. Sarusawa Pond, Nara ... *184*

80. Detail of courtyard garden, Yanagi-jaya restaurant, Nara ... *186*

81. Courtyard garden, Yanagi-jaya restaurant, Nara ... *187*

82, 83. Courtyard gardens, Suppon Dai-ichi restaurant, Kyoto ... *188*

84. Detail of courtyard garden, Suppon Dai-ichi restaurant, Kyoto ... *190*

85. Detail of courtyard garden, Takeka inn, Kyoto ... *191*

86. Second-floor view of courtyard garden, Takeka inn, Kyoto ... *192*

87. Courtyard garden, Sumiya, Kyoto ... *194*

88. Courtyard garden, Warajiya restaurant, Kyoto ... *196*

89. Courtyard garden, Shibata residence, Kyoto ... *197*

90. Front courtyard garden, Raku shop-residence, Kyoto ... *198*

91. Detail of courtyard garden, Zenta shop-residence, Kyoto ... *199*

92. Detail of courtyard garden in front of storehouse, Zenta shop-residence, Kyoto ... *200*

93. Courtyard garden, Onishi residence, Kyoto ... *201*

94. Detail of courtyard garden, Tabata residence, Kyoto   *202*

95. Stone wall and graveled path, Yoda residence, Kyoto   *203*

96. Rear garden, Yoda residence, Kyoto   *204*

97. Detail of courtyard garden, Uno residence, Kyoto   *206*

98. Steppingstones and garden shrubs, Uno residence, Kyoto   *207*

99. Front garden of Kato shop-residence, Kyoto   *208*

100. Courtyard garden, Kiyomizu shop-residence, Kyoto   *209*

101. Outer walls of Shinto priests' residences, Kamigamo Shrine, Kyoto   *210*

102. Front courtyard garden of Shinto priest's residence, Kamigamo Shrine, Kyoto   *211*

103. Detail of tea garden, Ura Senke, Kyoto   *212*

FOREWORD

T HIS BOOK deals chiefly with two distinctive types of the Japanese garden: the borrowed-landscape garden, which incorporates distant scenery as part of its design, and the small courtyard garden, which is generally enclosed by the component structures of a residence, a temple, a restaurant, or an inn. The tea garden, which strongly influenced the residential courtyard garden, is presented in an incidental role. Most of the gardens discussed here are in Kyoto.

The relationship between the borrowed-landscape garden and the tea garden is truly a strange one. The reason for this strangeness lies in the fact that the tea garden not only rejected the borrowed-landscape technique but also was a unique type of garden whose essential character predisposed it against the adoption of the technique. If we could place a borrowed-landscape garden and a tea garden next to each other and thereby closely observe the contrasts between them, the basic character of each would be thrown all the more into relief. At the same time we could no doubt trace something of the history of Kyoto and its surrounding area.

When I walk around Kyoto, I am constantly surprised. Hidden among the houses are courtyard gardens whose existence can hardly be surmised when one passes through the streets, and almost all of them display the influence of the tea garden. This phenomenon probably dates from some four hundred years ago, when the tea garden originated. Of course we also find borrowed-landscape gardens among the residences of Kyoto, but practically all of them date from no more than seventy-odd years ago, when modernization of the city got under way and when streetcars, new drainage systems, and the like made their appearance. At present, however, most gardens of these two types are gradually falling into decline. Since gardens are living things, they quickly go to ruin when they are neglected, and today the borrowed-landscape garden and the courtyard garden are by way of vanishing from the scene. Some front courtyard gardens are now used for the storage of tradesmen's goods; some inner courtyard gardens are perishing of neglect.

The gardens introduced in this book are for the most part privately owned. If it had not been for the courtesy and understanding of their owners, the book could never have been written, and I therefore wish to express my gratitude to these considerate people. I wish also to express my sincere thanks to Mr. Yoshikazu Muramatsu and Miss Fumiko Nakagawa, of the Tankosha publishing house, for their invaluable assistance in preparing the Japanese edition of the book.

It is pertinent to note here that in this book the names of all Japanese of the premodern (before 1868) period are given in Japanese style—that is, surname first—whereas those of Japanese of the modern period (after 1868) are given in Western style—that is, surname last.

TEIJI ITOH

SPACE AND ILLUSION IN
THE JAPANESE GARDEN

1: TO CAPTURE ALIVE

THE LITERAL MEANING of the Japanese word *shakkei* is "borrowed scenery" or "borrowed landscape"—that is, distant views incorporated into garden settings as part of the design. In its original sense, however, shakkei means neither a borrowed landscape nor a landscape that has been bought. It means a landscape captured alive. The distinction here is peculiarly Japanese, and it reflects the psychology of the garden designers. Its implications run more or less like this: when something is borrowed, it does not matter whether it is living or not, but when something is captured alive, it must invariably remain alive, just as it was before it was captured. Gardeners and nurserymen of former times, when they constructed borrowed-landscape gardens, never spoke of shakkei, for they considered the term inappropriate. From their point of view, every element of the design was a living thing: water, distant mountains, trees, and stones. Without a realization like this, it is impossible to perceive the essence of a borrowed-landscape garden or, for that matter, of a *tsuboniwa:* a courtyard (or enclosed) garden. Understanding of the term shakkei does not mean true understanding of the concept unless there is an actual sensation of what it signifies.

Something like the shakkei concept of using beautiful scenery beyond the actual confines of a garden had existed as early as the Heian period (794–1185), but it was not until the Muromachi period (1336–1568) that gardens recognizable as shakkei gardens began to appear and the style itself began to be established. And it was only at the beginning of the seventeenth century in China and in the nineteenth century in Japan that the term shakkei (in Chinese, *chieh-ching*) actually began to be used. In 1634, the same year in which the famous Japanese tea master and designer Kobori Enshu (1579–

1647) completed the teahouse at Nijo Castle in Kyoto and was placed in charge of constructing the Sento Imperial Palace garden in that city, there was published in Ming-dynasty China a book on landscape gardening by Li Chi-cheng (1582–?) called *Yuan-yeh* (in Japanese, *En'ya*). This work is a classic comparable to the immortal *Sakuteiki* (Treatise on Garden Making), written during the Heian period by the Japanese master Tachibana Toshitsuna (1027–94). In the last chapter of the *Yuan-yeh* the expression chieh-ching, or shakkei, appears for the first time.

Li Chi-cheng writes: "There are no particular rules for constructing a garden, but for the borrowing of landscapes there are certain techniques, and they are of the greatest importance in designing a garden with trees. The techniques are of four different types: borrowing from a great distance, borrowing from nearby, borrowing from a high level, and borrowing from a low level. Any one of these can be used according to the situation and the opportunities available." Nevertheless, Li gives us no particulars regarding shakkei techniques, and his book abounds with ornate and grandiose writing in the style of his time. To tell the truth, it was not this book that introduced the techniques of shakkei into Japan. It merely happened that the Japanese borrowed the term shakkei from the book during the Meiji (1868–1912) and Taisho (1912–1926) eras, when Japanese gardening techniques were being systematized in scholarly fashion, and it is therefore no wonder that the gardeners, who had no connection with academic learning, remained ignorant of the term, even though they had long been constructing gardens in shakkei style.

We do not know when the gardeners of Kyoto began to speak of the shakkei concept as *ikedori,* or "capturing alive." In any event, to make a landscape one's own by capturing it alive obviously requires a positive attitude toward scenery and a high degree of craftsmanship in garden design. Merely to choose a place with a good view, a place from which beautiful things can be seen, is decidedly not ikedori. A teahouse located in a mountain pass may command a splendid view of the world below, but such a view could never be called a borrowed landscape.

Still, it is impossible to construct a borrowed-landscape garden in an area where no attractive scenery exists. It is obvious that ugly and befouled scenery beyond the limits of the garden had better not be seen at all. Even today, in spite of much modern ugliness, the city of Kyoto is surrounded by scenery of great beauty, but, with few exceptions, it was only about a century ago that people began to incorporate this scenery into the design of their gardens.

The Heian-period aristocrats, for example, although they greatly admired beautiful scenery and traveled around the countryside to view it, made no effort to capture it alive in their gardens. The aristocrats of the preceding Nara period (646–794), dwelling in the capital that gave the period its name, expressed their love of natural beauty in poems that praised such nearby hills as Unebi, Miminashi, Kagu, Mikasa, Takamado, and Kasuga, but they did not incorporate vistas of these hills into their gardens. Instead they created miniature versions of remote places like Tamatsushima in Kii Province, the beach of Sumiyoshi, the islands of the Seto Inland Sea, Shiogama, and Matsushima. All these were places of great natural beauty where the sea played a major role in the setting, and they were all quite distant from the capital city of Nara. To visit them required days of travel on horseback or on foot over mountain after mountain, to say nothing of the risk of life in crossing open stretches of sea in a small boat.

2: TO COMMAND A GOOD VIEW

T HE YEAR WAS 1090, in the age when ostensibly retired emperors continued to rule from behind the scenes in the capital city of Kyoto while the throne itself was occupied by a succession of emperors who were only nominal rulers. The retired emperor Shirakawa (1053–1129), who then held the reins of government, one day asked the court nobleman Tachibana Toshitsuna to name for him the most outstanding among the famous gardens of the time. It was logical that such a request should be made of Toshitsuna, for he was not only the author of the previously noted *Treatise on Garden Making* but was also widely recognized as a true master of garden design. The retired emperor, not yet forty, was a man of great power who exercised control over the newly established class of wealthy provincial landowners upon whom he depended for financial support. Toshitsuna, on the other hand, was an old aristocrat who had already passed the age of sixty and had no political power.

The first garden that Toshitsuna named in answer to Shirakawa's inquiry was the garden of the Ishida villa. The second was that of the Kaya-in, the former residence of Toshitsuna's deceased father, Fujiwara Yorimichi (992–1074). In his *Treatise on Garden Making,* Toshitsuna tells us that in 1021, when the Kaya-in garden was under construction, Yorimichi could find no designer whom he considered sufficiently expert in the placement of stones and, since there was nothing else to be done, supervised the construction himself. It is thought that the Kaya-in, after Yorimichi's death in 1074, came into the possession of his son Morozane.

The real reason for the retired emperor Shirakawa's inquiry was that he himself had designed a garden and naturally expected it to be named among

Toshitsuna's choices. This was the garden of the immense detached palace that had been completed for the emperor in 1086 at Toba, in the southern suburbs of Kyoto, and occupied a site running some 654 meters east to west and some 872 meters north to south. The residence was known as the Toba Palace.

After hearing Toshitsuna's first two choices, the retired emperor became impatient and said: "The third one must surely be the garden of the Toba Palace." But Toshitsuna's answer was unexpectedly blunt. "To be sure," he said, "the Toba Palace and its garden were built under Your Majesty's supervision, but the topographical view there is quite commonplace. I regret to say it, but the third choice must be the garden of my own Fushimi Pavilion."

This story comes from the *Imakagami,* a chronicle dealing mainly with court events from around 1025 to 1170, the year when it was completed. The *Imakagami* goes on to say that there were some people who disagreed with Toshitsuna's choice of the Kaya-in garden and offered the opinion that he should have named instead the Byodo-in, the celebrated villa built by his father at Uji and still extant today. In any event, it is interesting to surmise why Toshitsuna dared to omit from his choices of outstanding gardens the one at the imposing palace of so powerful a man as Shirakawa. To begin with, both his father, Yorimichi, and his elder brother, Morozane, had served Shirakawa in the capacity of *kampaku,* or chief adviser, and it is therefore most likely that Toshitsuna himself was on intimate terms with the emperor. The most important reason for his boldness, however, must have been his own discerning knowledge of garden design and the self-confidence that it engendered.

Still, the fact that his father had attained the influential position of kampaku did not open the way to political advancement for Toshitsuna, most probably because his mother did not come from a family of sufficiently high social position. After his father's death, when his mother married Tachibana Toshinori, lord of Sanuki Province in Shikoku, he became a member of the Tachibana family. Unlike his brother Morozane, who advanced to the level of kampaku, Toshitsuna barely managed to become a high steward in Owari Province and thus, in spite of having the blood of the illustrious Fujiwara family in his veins, had to content himself with an obscure political position. It was undoubtedly these circumstances that turned him in the direction of garden design. Just as it was the sons and daughters of lower-level noblemen who brought Heian literature to flower, so it was this politically obscure outsider of a man who laid one of the earliest foundation stones of Japanese garden art.

What immediately calls for attention in the episode from the *Imakagami* is the clear evidence that Toshitsuna conceived of a garden in terms of its environment. His opinion concerning the garden of the Toba Palace is significant because it suggests that he never appraised a garden purely on its own intrinsic merits, no matter how perfect it might be. Certainly he must have recognized the excellence of the garden itself. The only drawback was the plainness of the topographical view. The Toba area was flat, and there were no mountains or hills nearby—no scenery to compare with the river and the hills that formed the setting of the Byodo-in at Uji or with the hillside backdrop of Toshitsuna's Fushimi Pavilion.

Some people cite this story from the *Imakagami* as evidence that the concept of shakkei already existed during the closing years of the Heian period, but it would be carrying one's thinking too far to conclude that garden techniques had been classified to that extent in Heian times. Nowhere in the story is it implied that Toshitsuna excluded the Toba Palace garden from his selection of the finest gardens because it neglected the shakkei technique and did not borrow a beautiful landscape. It is simply stated that the Toba Palace was located in a topographically flat area. Nor does Toshitsuna himself, in his *Treatise on Garden Making*, ever mention the concept of shakkei. We can assume that the Heian aristocrats showed an interest in the environment of a garden site and in the views that the site commanded, and we know definitely that Tachibana Toshitsuna, as the pioneer critic of garden garden design, showed such an interest. At the same time, however, it is only correct to assume that the technique of incorporating an exterior view into the garden design by treating the garden and the view as a single entity had not really been established.

Toshitsuna's Fushimi Pavilion, whose garden he named as his third choice, was unsurpassed in its elegance. Here hillside paths formed part of the garden setting, and we are told that arriving guests were met by a guide in traveling costume who led them to the pavilion itself. Unlike the gardens of noblemen's mansions within the city limits of Kyoto, this one suggested a rural garden in a mountain village. But the Fushimi Pavilion burned down toward the close of 1093, and its garden was destroyed along with it. Fujiwara Munetada lamented the disaster in his diary the *Chuyuki:* "The streams and the rocks there were mysteriously elegant. Now everything is turned to ashes. It is truly a regrettable loss." The next year, having become seriously ill, Toshitsuna renounced the world and entered the Buddhist priesthood. In the summer of that year he died at the age of sixty-six, and the site of the Fushimi Pavilion came into the possession of his brother Morozane. Later, at the request of the retired emperor Shirakawa, a palace known as the Sento Gosho (a generic name for the palaces of retired emperors) was erected there. Still later it became the site of the Fushimi Palace.

During the succeeding Kamakura period (1185–1336) the view from the garden of the Fushimi Palace became more and more a point of interest among the aristocracy. In the autumn of 1279 the retired emperors Gofuka-kusa and Kameyama journeyed to the palace in ox-drawn carriages to enjoy the scenery of the surrounding hills. We can imagine the charm of the scene as the court nobles and officials of the emperors' retinue, all in informal costume of various styles, gathered here and there to frolic in the midst of full-blooming chrysanthemums and scarlet maple trees. Looking out from the palace and its garden, one saw a panorama of autumn-tinted fields and hills through which the Uji River, its ripples sparkling in the sunlight, flowed toward the towns of Fushimi and Yamada. It was a view of unexcelled beauty, and we are told that the young courtiers, especially, were enthralled by it.

On an evening late in the next year the court held a Buddhist memorial service at the Fushimi Palace, and a description of the garden on that occasion survives in the diary of one of the courtiers who took part in the ceremony. It was an evening of brilliant moonlight, the diary tells us, and everything seemed to be clothed in white. The leaves of the trees and shrubs could almost have been taken for flowers, and the pond, shining like a mirror, had a special elegance of its own. There was a peculiar charm in the withered grasses that bent sadly down around its edges. In the great quietude there was no sound but that of water flowing among the rocks, and only the pine trees touching the eaves of the palace "had a heartless look about them," the diary interestingly notes.

Nevertheless, for all its quiet elegance and its view of surrounding hills and fields, this garden had not been constructed with the idea of incorporating such exterior scenery. It was simply a garden that depended upon its own intrinsic refinement and nothing more.

As the city of Kyoto (then called Heian-kyo) increased the pace of its urbanization, it gradually became more difficult to construct the traditional pond garden of the nobleman's residence within the city limits, not only because of straitened financial conditions among the aristocrats but also because of the shortage of water, occasioned by the overcutting of mountain forests where the sources of water existed. In fact, the water shortage had become drastic even as early as the mid-twelfth century. According to a record of the times, in 1149 the pond at the Higashi Sanjo Palace, residence of the head of the powerful Fujiwara family, had dried up to the extent that not even a ripple could be seen upon it. The courtier Tomotaka, an official in charge of protocol for imperial visits, ordered the police commissioners to fill the pond in preparation for a visit by the emperor, but there was no water to be had, and it was truly an indignity, the record notes, to have nothing but an empty pond when the emperor arrived. From time immemorial the Higashi Sanjo Palace had had countless springs within its grounds, but now even the garden of the foremost court nobleman had come to this sorry pass, and it is easy to imagine what the shortage of water had done to the gardens of less influential aristocrats.

Outside the capital, however, and not too distant from it, there were still such beautiful and relatively undeveloped stretches of plain as Saga, Uda, and Ohara. As the nearby hills and mountains changed color from season to season, it was only natural that the court aristocrats, in their untiring pursuit of elegance, should take intense pleasure in the superb scenery that could be viewed there from their mansions and villas.

Here we must once again make a clear distinction: a garden that commands a good view is one thing, but a shakkei garden is quite another. Naturally, if there is no good view from the site, a shakkei garden cannot be constructed, but a good view from the garden does not signify that the shakkei technique was employed. The Yoshino Detached Palace, built in 656, the second year of the empress Saimei's reign, stood in a setting that clearly suggested the scenery of the Chinese mountain Kushe-t'ai (in Japanese, Koya-dai), where Taoist "immortals" were said to dwell. There were countless waterfalls, and mountain torrents dashed through the rocks. There was an incomparable beauty in the quiet, secluded valleys, but in no sense could any of this be called borrowed scenery. It was simply that the natural setting there was the garden itself and that exterior landscape was not captured alive for the sake of a garden adjoining the palace.

The Otsu Palace of the emperor Tenji, erected in 667, was of this same order, as was the detached palace built for the emperor Shomu at Tamatsu-shima in 724 and memorialized in the following poem from the Nara-period anthology *Man'yoshu:*

It was good to look upon Tamatsushima,
But now I am no longer there,
And in the capital I long for it.

Tamatsushima was on the seacoast in Kii Province (the present Wakayama
Prefecture), and we can readily assume that the maritime scenery of Waka-
noura was the sole object of its garden. Similarly, the villa built for the same
emperor on Mount Takamado, east of the city of Nara, employed the view
from there as the very purpose of its garden. But in none of these instances
can we speak of the garden as a shakkei garden.

As we have already seen, the court noblemen of the Nara and Heian
periods, although they admired the scenery in the vicinity of the cities of
Nara and Kyoto, were not sufficiently interested in it to reproduce it in
their gardens. Instead, what they attempted to copy there was the scenery
of remote places that had achieved fame through the descriptions of travelers.
The most typical of such gardens in the early Heian period was the one at
the Rokujo Kawara-in, the Kyoto residence of the important government
minister Minamoto Toru (822–95). Its scenery copied that of two celebrated locales in the province of Rikuzen (the present Miyagi Prefecture)
in northern Honshu: the beach of Shiogama, where salt was refined, and the
pine-clad islands of Matsushima. The pond was dotted with miniature islands,
and salt pans were placed here and there at the edge of the water, their smoke
rising into the sky. Both the earlier capital, Nara, and the later capital, Kyoto,
were surrounded by hills and mountains, and it seems only natural that
what the court noblemen reproduced in their gardens was not this familiar
scenery but scenery that had claimed the admiration of government officials
assigned to distant provinces in Japan or dispatched as envoys to T'ang China
—in a word, scenery that could not be viewed in either of the two capital
cities. This exclusive predilection for the landscapes of remote places as
subjects for garden design continued throughout the early Heian period.

But even after the middle of the Heian period, when the aristocrats at last
began to show interest in scenery closer at hand, the scenery of distant regions
continued to fascinate them. We learn from extant records, for example,
that the garden at the Higashi Rokujo-in, residence of the government
minister Sukechika, contained a miniature copy of Ama no Hashidate (Bridge
of Heaven), the famous scenic spot that lies northwest of Kyoto on the Sea
of Japan. We also learn that around 1035 the garden of Taira Narichika, near

the Toba Palace, had a pond with a sandy beach that imitated the scenery of Sumiyoshi, in Osaka, and that people of the time spoke of Narichika's residence as the Sumiyoshi Palace or the Sandy Beach Palace.

When we come to the subject of borrowed scenery in the gardens of Kyoto, we are most likely to think of such scenic landmarks as Mount Hiei and the Eastern Hills (Higashiyama), but in past ages, when first Nara and then Kyoto flourished as the capital, a view of mountains from the garden was never considered a motif in garden design. As we have observed before, the Nara aristocrats composed poems about the six noted hills of the province in which their capital lay, but they made no connection between these hills and the design of their gardens. The fact that gardens were often called *shima,* or islands, in the Asuka period (552–646), as well as in the Nara and Heian periods, makes it clear that the main objective in garden construction in those times was the reproduction of seacoast scenery. In the eighth-century *Nihon Shoki* (Chronicles of Japan) we read, for example, that in the early seventh century the influential government minister Soga Umako had a garden in which there was a small pond with a small island and that Umako was therefore called the Lord of the Island. Similarly, among the poems in the *Man'yoshu* there are many in which "island" is a synonym for "garden," and in the *Ise Monogatari* (Tales of Ise), dating from the early Heian period, we find a "lord who loves an island"—that is, a lord who loves a garden.

In any event, when was it that the long-neglected hills and mountains were taken up as an object of garden design? And which garden was it that first employed the shakkei technique? Here we must recall the garden of the Tenryu-ji, the fourteenth-century temple at Arashiyama in Kyoto.

The Tenryu-ji was founded in 1345 by the military ruler Ashikaga Takauji, who, acting on the advice of the Buddhist priest Muso Soseki, undertook to establish it as a memorial temple for the deceased emperor Godaigo and for the warriors who died in the civil strife that brought Takauji to power. The construction of the temple required some four years, beginning in 1341, when Muso Soseki officiated at the groundbreaking ceremony. Since 1341 was the fourth year of the Ryakuo era under the short-lived Northern dynasty of emperors, the temple was first given the name Ryakuo-ji, but the powerful priests and monks of the Enryaku-ji on Mount Hiei, a temple also named for an era, issued a strong protest, and the name was then changed to Tenryu-ji.

We know quite well that the Tenryu-ji garden borrows the scenery of the two hills Arashiyama and Kameyama—in particular, that of Arashiyama

(Plates 30–33). Although the temple was completed early in the period of the Northern and Southern courts, when, for some fifty-eight years, Japan had two emperors simultaneously, there had already been a garden on the site from early Heian times. This garden, however, had not borrowed the scenery of Arashiyama. The emperor Daigo, who reigned from 897 to 930, had a talented son, Prince Kaneakira (914–87), who excelled in scholarship, achieved considerable mastery in literature and calligraphy, and is represented by poems in several extant anthologies. The land on which the Tenryu-ji stands today was once the site of Kaneakira's villa, and we learn from his poem in praise of the god of Kameyama that his garden had a pond fed by water from a spring on the hill. Kameyama means Tortoise Hill, and, as the name implies, the hill is a rather low one in the shape of a tortoise. There is a further suggestion in the name that the hill was thought of as a kind of Mount Horai, a seagirt mountain in the Taoist paradise.

Like Arashiyama, Kameyama at this time was not an object of the borrowed-scenery technique. Instead, as we have just noted, it appears to have represented a *shinsen-to*—that is, an unearthly mountain island in a mythical sea. The Taoist concept of an unearthly land where immortals dwell had been introduced into Japan as early as the Asuka period, but it was not until the Heian period—the time of Prince Kaneakira—that Taoist ideas began to influence garden design. We find examples of this influence in descriptions of the garden of the Toba Palace, which had an "unearthly island," and of the military leader Taira Kiyomori's garden of artemisia at his Nishi Hachijo Palace. But at Prince Kaneakira's villa the concept of the unearthly island, or Mount Horai, was not used to symbolize eternity. Instead, the hill called Kameyama represented the old Japanese belief that the tortoise lived to the age of ten thousand years and was therefore a felicitous symbol. This fact attests to a considerable Japanization of Taoist ideas of an unearthly land. Still, even though Kameyama symbolized felicity, it is only proper to assume that there was no shakkei garden at the site of the Tenryu-ji in Prince Kaneakira's day.

For some three centuries after the prince's death, the villa and its site were allowed to fall more and more deeply into desolation. Then, in the Kamakura period, the retirement palace of the former emperor Gosaga (1220–72) was built there. According to the *Godai Teio Monogatari* (Stories of Five Emperors), Gosaga moved to this new residence at the foot of Kameyama after his Gojo Palace in the heart of Kyoto had twice been destroyed by fire, once in 1257 and then, after it had been reconstructed, once again in 1270. He named his new residence the Kameyama Palace and lived there for the rest of his life. We learn that one of the retired emperors visited the palace in the summer of 1276 and composed a poem to commemorate the occasion:

Eternity
And the pine trees on Tortoise Hill
Reflected in the clear waters
Of the palace pond.

By combining the auspicious images of the tortoise and pine trees, both of which symbolize long life, the poem quite clearly expresses good wishes for the owner of the garden, and its concept is unmistakably that of the Japanized unearthly land.

The garden of the Kameyama Palace is frequently the theme of poems in a number of the imperial anthologies, but there is no mention at all of Arashiyama. It is obvious that the concept of the unearthly land of the immortals had formed itself around the image of Kameyama, just as it is obvious that Arashiyama, at this time, was a matter of no interest, let alone a matter of consideration as borrowed scenery.

In the following Muromachi period, when the Kameyama Palace gave way to the Tenryu-ji, Arashiyama made its first appearance as part of the garden scenery. In 1344 the main gate of the temple, the large triple gate, and the lecture hall were still under construction. The garden, however, must have been nearly completed, for in the autumn of that year the retired emperor Kogon of the Northern dynasty visited there to enjoy the splendid landscape of Arashiyama. No doubt the garden pond, which now extended out in front of the abbot's quarters at the foot of Kameyama, had been redesigned by Muso Soseki from the pond that existed there in the days of the Kameyama Palace, but what calls for attention here is Arashiyama itself.

The shogun Ashikaga Takauji had this hill planted with cherry trees from Yoshino and maple trees from along the Tatsuta River. It was in the Yoshino region of Yamato Province (the present Nara Prefecture) that Godaigo, as the first emperor of the Southern dynasty, had built his palace, and the cherry trees were transplanted from there. Like the mountains of Yoshino, Arashiyama has been renowned for its cherry blossoms from that day on. At the same time, it came to be captured alive as a feature of the garden in front of the abbot's quarters at the Tenryu-ji. In earlier days it had been nothing more than part of the surrounding scenery and had not been made a feature of the garden composition. It is even possible to think that Arashiyama could not have been seen at all from the garden of the Kameyama Palace if the trees in the garden had formed a tall enough screen to block it from view. If the elegantly simple arrangement of rocks on the opposite bank of the pond in the Tenryu-ji garden suggests a landscape painting in the Chinese style of the Northern Sung dynasty, the view of Arashiyama with its cherry trees in full bloom seems more than anything else to resemble a painting in the traditional Japanese *yamato-e* style.

It was only after the building of the Tenryu-ji that Arashiyama became an attraction. Kameyama, which had once served as an auspicious symbol of an unearthly realm, at last faded from prominence, and Arashiyama, rising behind it, dominated the view. With its cherry blossoms in spring and its brilliant maple leaves in autumn, it had been captured alive for the garden in front of the abbot's quarters. Two years after the Tenryu-ji was completed, in the spring of 1347, the retired emperor Kogon visited there to view the cherry blossoms of Arashiyama at the height of their beauty, enjoying the scene from the senior priest's chamber.

But it was not only in spring that Arashiyama transformed itself into a splendid sight. In the autumn of 1464 the eighth Ashikaga shogun, Yoshimasa, made an excursion to the Tenryu-ji to enjoy the view of the borrowed scenery of Arashiyama and its scarlet maple trees from the Dragon's Gate Pavilion. Muso Soseki himself, who motivated the construction of the Tenryu-ji, once composed a poem as he viewed snow-covered Arashiyama from the abbot's quarters of the temple:

> Arashiyama, white with snow,
> Almost seems to be
> Engulfed in clouds of flowers.
> Pine trees, by a magic touch,
> Transfigured into cherry trees.

So it was that Arashiyama, captured alive for the Tenryu-ji garden, put on new colors with the changing seasons.

It seems that the Togetsu Bridge over the nearby Oi River (now called the Oseki River) was also once part of the captured scenery, for a map drawn in 1426 shows that the Tenryu-ji compound extended quite close to the river and that there were no houses between the compound and the river, as there are today. Also, at that time, the Togetsu Bridge was located farther upstream and could be seen from the compound.

All too often the Tenryu-ji had to suffer devastation by fire and civil war. As early as the spring of 1358 its main buildings were lost in a fire, and during the succeeding century or so it went through no fewer than six destructive conflagrations. Inevitably the garden itself underwent certain changes as a result of these disasters.

Again, as the trees planted at the far side of the garden gradually grew taller, they obscured the view of Arashiyama. People knew more or less by hearsay that Arashiyama had once formed the borrowed scenery of the garden, but long years were to pass before it was restored to that role. On September 21, 1934, a storm of unprecedented violence in the Kyoto region brought down all the overgrown trees in the garden, and Arashiyama once again revealed itself in front of the Tenryu-ji.

The arrangement of rocks in the foreground of the garden, suggestive of a Chinese landscape painting in the Northern Sung style, as we have noted, may seem to combine rather oddly with the borrowed scenery of Arashiyama, which is reminiscent of painting in the traditional Japanese style. Still, the contrast here is one of considerable interest. The view of Arashiyama, which until Muromachi times had been ignored as a possible element in the design of the garden, came to have both pictorial and historical importance, attracting people to the Tenryu-ji and impressing them, particularly through the superb sight of the cherry trees from Yoshino and the maple trees from the banks of the Tatsuta River. The view from the abbot's quarters and the guest room of the temple, employing the compositional techniques of painting, embraces both the garden and the hill beyond and thus in itself becomes a kind of painting.

There is no way of knowing whether or not the garden of the Tenryu-ji was the first garden in shakkei style. It seems quite natural, however, that the shakkei concept should not have existed in the Nara and Heian periods, when people were interested only in copying seacoast scenery in their gardens or in constructing them as representations of the Buddhist paradise, for gardens of these two types had no relationship at all with the scenery beyond their boundaries. If we assume that a firm farewell to such ancient concepts of garden making was a prerequisite for the emergence of the shakkei style, there was ample possibility that the shakkei garden would make its appearance early in the Muromachi period, for it was then that Japanese landscape painting entered a new phase of development. And, as we can see in the example of the Tenryu-ji garden, the shakkei style of the early period made great use of the compositional techniques of painting.

3: TO CONSTITUTE A
SHAKKEI GARDEN

WHEN WE STUDY existing shakkei gardens, we discover that there are techniques common to all of them. We also discover that the gardens have certain essentials in common.

The first of these essentials is that the garden be within the premises of a building or a complex of buildings. It does not matter if it is an enclosed, or interior, garden rather than an open one, although enclosed shakkei gardens are extremely rare. Nor does it matter what basic form the garden takes. It may be a garden of nothing but stones and gravel like the garden of the abbot's quarters at the Ryoan-ji in Kyoto, or it may be a garden planted with trees and shrubbery to create a woodland effect. Again, it may be a symbolic garden suggestive of Buddhist teachings, or it may be a realistic garden with quite natural landscapes. Or, to cite one more example of contrasting forms, it may be a garden designed to be viewed from a static position (as on a veranda) and to induce meditation, or it may be a stroll garden: a garden in which one can admire a succession of changing views as he walks along its paths.

Nevertheless, there is one type of garden that does not make use of borrowed scenery. This is the tea garden. We do not know of a single tea garden in shakkei style, and we may quite reasonably ask why this should be so. Is it because the tea garden is normally quite small and is often located in crowded city areas where it is impossible to employ shakkei techniques? To be sure, this could be one of the reasons, but smallness in itself is no obstacle to the use of borrowed scenery. For example, the shakkei garden of the Joju-in (Plates 28, 29), in the precincts of the Kiyomizu Temple in Kyoto, is no larger than the garden of the Yabunouchi school of tea in the same city

(Plates 69, 70). The chief reason why the tea garden rejects borrowed scenery is that it is not designed to be looked at from the tearoom or the teahouse. Its purpose, rather, is to serve as a forestage on which the prologue to the tea ceremony itself takes place. In other words, the *roji,* or "dewy path," through the tea garden to the *nijiri-guchi,* the low sliding-door aperture by which the guests enter the teahouse, is an approach that induces a properly contemplative mood for the occasion. The guests are in fact the actors on this forestage, and there is no need for borrowed scenery, which in any event would distract them from the mood that the tea garden seeks to create. As the last guest enters the teahouse, he closes the door of the nijiri-guchi behind him, and the sound of its closing is the cue for the host to begin the tea ceremony. It is therefore quite clear that the garden is not meant to be viewed from the teahouse. In this respect, shakkei gardens and tea gardens stand diametrically opposed to each other.

The second essential of the shakkei garden is the borrowed scenery itself: the object to be captured alive. By far the most common among the objects of capture are mountains and hills. In Kyoto, where the shakkei garden originated, these were most typically Mount Hiei, the Higashiyama range, the Nishiyama range (including Arashiyama), and Otokoyama. In Edo (present-day Tokyo), Mount Fuji, though some ninety-six kilometers distant, was a favorite object of the borrowed-scenery technique, and in Shiga Prefecture, north of Kyoto, Mount Ibuki played the same role. But plains were also included among the natural features that were captured by shakkei gardens. In fact, they were second only to mountains and hills in this respect. For example, the east garden of the Jiko-in, a temple in Nara Prefecture, has a shakkei view of the Yamato Plain (Plates 2, 34–36). Similarly, marine landscapes have been captured, as in the garden of the Koki-an in Odawara (Kanagawa Prefecture). Still other gardens have made use of waterfalls, lakes, marshes, woods, and forests as borrowed features of scenic design. Again, man-made objects may become elements of borrowed scenery. The garden of the Shinshin-an in Kyoto (Plates 24–27), for example, incorporates a view of the triple gate and the bell tower of the great Zen temple Nanzen-ji, while the Isui-en garden in Nara (Plates 37–39) offers an imposing vista of the Great South Gate of the Todai-ji. Buddha halls, pagodas, and other beautiful structures will serve just as well, and in rare instances even an imperial tomb may constitute the borrowed scenery, as it does in the garden of the Yojuro Yasuda residence in Kyoto, which embraces a view of the tomb of Emperor Montoku, dating from the ninth century. To capture an imperial tomb as borrowed scenery is in a certain sense a wise choice. Other vistas, whether natural or man-made, can change or disappear despite all intentions to capture and preserve them alive, for garden owners have no control over their existence. Under present law, however, it is highly improbable that any imperial tomb will be changed in any way. We also learn that some shakkei gardens have been designed to capture the nighttime fire lures of fishermen, but such borrowed scenery is unstable indeed, for its existence is always threatened by changes in fishing methods as well as by the vicissitudes of the fishing industry itself.

The third essential of the garden in shakkei style is *mikiri,* or trimming: the device by which the garden designer limits the borrowed landscape to the features he wishes to show. In many ways it is the same sort of trimming that one undertakes with a photographic enlargement to eliminate the irrelevant portions. When we view a potential borrowed landscape from a position near the foreground of a garden—perhaps from a veranda—we often see features in it that are not wanted in the shakkei design. To conceal these irrelevant or undesirable features, trimming is needed, and for this purpose low clay walls topped with tile are commonly used, since they function most reliably as screens to block the view. Fences and thin hedges are unsuitable because they have openings through which unwanted parts of the borrowed landscape can still be seen. Thick and luxuriant hedges, carefully pruned, are quite appropriate, as can be seen in such instances as the hedge in the east garden of the abbot's residence at the Daitoku-ji in Kyoto and the double hedge of Japanese cypress in the east garden of the Koho-an at that temple. Such hedges are usually composed of mixed plantings. For example, the one at the Entsu-ji (also in Kyoto) makes use of such plants as the camellia, sasanqua, tea bush, gardenia, oak, and Chinese hawthorn. The above-mentioned hedge in the east garden of the abbot's residence at the Daitoku-ji is a double one whose lower part consists of camellia, oak, and *nezumi-mochi* (a species of camellia). If a hedge is made up of only one species of plant, it tends to attract the viewer's eye and at the same time to distract his attention from the distant scenery beyond it. Mixed plantings, on the other hand, have a suitably vague and unobtrusive character, and this is no doubt the reason why they have traditionally been used. Here we most decidedly have an example of the refinement of technique.

There is another method of trimming that uses neither walls nor pruned hedges but, instead, conceals unwanted parts of the borrowed landscape behind an earthen embankment or the shoulder of an elevation in the garden terrain—for example, a low man-made hill. When this technique is employed, the slope is given a natural irregular appearance, planted with grass and shrubs, and ornamented here and there with rocks so placed as to seem part of the original terrain. The ridge of the slope then becomes the trimming line for the borrowed scenery. The previously mentioned garden of the Koki-an demonstrates this technique of limiting the borrowed scenery.

To summarize, the techniques of mikiri, or trimming, are of three types: the type that uses low clay walls, the type that uses pruned hedges, and the type that uses low hills or embankments. It must be noted, however, that trimming is not merely a matter of hiding unwanted scenery. The difficult part of the process lies in the need to make an effective capture of the scenery that is actually wanted.

The fourth essential of the shakkei garden is the linking of the borrowed scenery with the foreground of the garden by means of intermediary objects. In the previously described Tenryu-ji garden, the arrangement of rocks on the far side of the pond, suggesting a painting in Chinese style, serves as a link between the foreground (the near side of the pond) and the borrowed scenery of Arashiyama, which in turn suggests a painting in traditional Japanese style.

When the gardeners of Kyoto used the expression "to capture alive," they invariably implied the question "To capture alive with what?" The "what" in this question is the element that brings the borrowed scenery into the garden. If we use fishing as an analogy, the "what" corresponds to the net, the rod, the octopus trap, or some similar device. In other words, the fourth essential of shakkei design is the means by which the garden captures the distant scenery: trees, the sky, a stone lantern, a pillar or a post in a building, or a window. This capturing device, which usually occupies the space that seems to lie midway between the foreground and the background of the garden, can perhaps be described as middle-ground scenery. The chief function of the middle-ground scenery, then, is to bring together the more distant scenery and the forefront of the garden in one integrated vista. By such means, even a small garden can be transfigured into a garden of greater spaciousness and depth. In the following six chapters we shall observe the main techniques by which borrowed scenery is captured and made a living part of the garden.

4: TO CAPTURE WITH TREE TRUNKS

As one gets off the bus at Mizoro Pond, the last stop on the line, and enters the hillside path that runs along the Kurama Highway, he finds it hard to believe that he is still in Kyoto. Looking back, he sees the old capital itself lying below in the hazy distance. Then, after a fifteen-minute walk, he comes to the hilltop village of Hataeda. Here, in 1648, during the early years of the Edo period (1603–1868), a villa was built for the retired emperor Gomizuno-o (1596–1680). This event took place before the building of the emperor's celebrated villa Shugaku-in, about which more will be said in a later chapter.

The villa at Hataeda was known as the Hataeda Palace or the Hataeda Teahouse, the latter name deriving from the fact that "teahouse" (*chaya*) in this case was a term of rather broad meaning that included residences of the villa type. Several other buildings, also called teahouses, were built between the foot of the hill and the top. The plan here was similar to that of the subsequently constructed Shugaku-in garden, with its lower, middle, and upper levels, but the shortage of water in the area prevented the building of a pond like the one at Shugaku-in.

A decade or so later, around 1659, the Shugaku-in villa was completed, and the one at Hataeda was no longer used by the emperor. In 1672, with the exception of the palace building itself, the hill and the teahouses were given to the Konoe family as an imperial grant, and in 1678 the palace building became the temple known as the Entsu-ji. The present Buddha hall of the temple is a building that was transported there in the same year from the grounds of the Kyoto Imperial Palace. Today the temple compound is smaller than it was at that time, for an illustration in the contemporary

Miyako Meisho Zue (Pictures of Famous Places in the Capital) shows it to have been fairly extensive.

The garden of the Entsu-ji (Plates 17–19) is a small moss garden with a hummocky terrain and some forty stones and clumps of shrubbery, all carefully laid out but completely natural in appearance. The stones, set low in the ground, seem to be natural outcrops. The trimming line for the borrowed scenery is a thickly grown hedge beyond which the slope of the hill is planted mainly with a luxuriant grove of bamboo. In early autumn the air is filled with the singing of cicadas: the only sound to break the wonderful silence of the place.

The borrowed scenery of the garden is a distant view of Mount Hiei. Since the mountain is some six kilometers to the east, its forested slopes appear to have a bluish cast, and its creases are blurred, so that only the main contours are clear. The color of the mountain changes from day to day and from season to season and is particularly fine in the morning and the evening. Long ago, it is said, the spire of the West Pagoda of the Enryaku-ji could be seen sparkling in the evening sun at the summit of the mountain. Most unforgettable of all, however, is the view of Mount Hiei from the garden of the Entsu-ji on a moonlit night. One is made to wonder whether the garden and its borrowed scenery are the same today as they were in the past, but of course time moves stealthily and relentlessly on, and today, near the western peak of the mountain, one can see electric lights twinkling after the sun goes down.

Still, as we have observed several times before, a splendid view does not in itself constitute borrowed scenery, and a view of Mount Hiei alone does not mean that the mountain landscape has been captured alive. The garden of the Entsu-ji does capture the mountain alive, however, by letting us view it through the middle-ground scenery of several cryptomeria and Japanese cypress trees whose trunks, in effect, serve to draw it into the garden design. The scene almost literally becomes a painting, for it, too, is a pictorial composition.

A few of the trees are planted inside the hedge that forms the trimming line, but most of them stand just beyond it. These several cryptomerias and cypresses serve to link Mount Hiei to the foreground of the garden. By means of such a simple device the view from the Entsu-ji is saved from being just an ordinary vista. At the same time, Mount Hiei is saved from being nothing more than a background for the garden. Indeed, the cryptomerias and cypresses in the middle ground capture the mountain alive.

Among these large and sturdy trees, which soar straight upward, there is a single red pine whose slender and twisted trunk makes it seem strangely out of place: an alien among these strong links that draw Mount Hiei into the garden. Judging by its small girth, one must conclude that it grew from a seedling that sprouted there some fifty or sixty years ago. In any case, it is regrettable that this red pine somewhat disturbs the harmony of the scene, even though, as we shall presently see, it would not be out of place in a group of its own species used for the same purpose.

The device of capturing a distant mountain alive by letting it be viewed through a grouping of trees is the most common of shakkei techniques. The trees that are used as links between the borrowed scenery and the foreground of the garden must be fairly large, and their lowest branches must be high above the ground, since it is their trunks through which the scenery is viewed. Trees whose branches begin near the ground are useless, since they obstruct a distant view. Again, because the trees are large and quite close to the viewer, their trunks must have a beautiful texture. One tree that satisfies all these conditions is the red pine. If a somewhat stronger accent is desired for the intermediary scenery, the black pine will serve equally well. When the distant view is grand in scale, zelkovas and evergreen oaks are probably the best choices. Cryptomerias can also be used satisfactorily if they are of a type whose branches are sufficiently high above the ground. Of course, either transplanted trees or trees already growing on the site can be used as intermediary scenery in this shakkei technique.

The east garden of the abbot's residence at the Daitoku-ji, also in shakkei style, was constructed around the same time as the garden of the Entsu-ji. Like the adjoining south garden, it is spread with white gravel, but its stones are fewer in number and are arranged in a traditional pattern of three groups made up of seven, five, and three stones respectively. Although the pattern thus calls for a total of fifteen stones, one more stone has somehow become part of the arrangement. It is possible that the sixteen stones were meant to symbolize the Sixteen Arhats, or original disciples of the Buddha, but such speculations need not detain us here.

This garden, like that of the Entsu-ji, uses the trunks of large trees to capture Mount Hiei. The links in this case are two zelkovas and one *muku,* a species of elm. Of the two parallel hedges that form the trimming line, the one at the rear, consisting of evergreen oak, is the taller, but in former times it was undoubtedly lower or perhaps did not exist at all. It is most likely that the hedge was allowed to grow taller in order to obscure the roofs of houses that gradually encroached upon the area to the east of the Daitoku-ji. But today the houses rise above the hedge, and the shakkei composition has been destroyed. To speak metaphorically, although the meshes of the net for capturing scenery alive have still not been torn, it becomes increasingly difficult to accomplish the capture. In other words, the devices are still valid, but it is now almost impossible to conceal unwanted scenery by means of conventional trimming methods. If the hedge were allowed to grow taller, the harmony would be lost, and only the tip of Mount Hiei could be seen. It appears that there is no way of recovering the shakkei view. The great storm of 1934 that brought down the obstructing trees and restored the borrowed scenery of Arashiyama to the Tenryu-ji garden was indeed a *kamikaze:* a divine wind like the one that destroyed the invading Mongol fleet and saved Japan in the thirteenth century. But it seems unlikely that the Daitoku-ji, surrounded now on all sides by the invading city, will ever receive a similar blessing from a divine wind.

If we speak of Mount Hiei as now having all but fled from the abbot's garden at the Daitoku-ji, then we must say that the hill once held captive by the garden of the Ryoan-ji has long since completely escaped. This celebrated Kyoto garden, a creation consisting of nothing but fifteen stones set in a bed of fine white gravel, is a typical *sekitei,* or stone garden, in Zen style. There are some who say that it was constructed around the end of the fifteenth century, while others believe that it dates from the early seventeenth century, but neither of these opinions is particularly relevant here. Again, according to one popular belief, the garden was designed by the artist Soami (?–1525), while another attributes it to the Zen priest Hannyabo Tessen, and a certain novel, taking its cue from the names of two men carved on one of the stones, ascribes it to the "riverbed workmen" Kotaro and Seijiro. Such suppositions, however, like those concerning the date of the garden, have no bearing on the present discussion.

Beyond the low tile-topped wall that marks the south edge of the garden, there is a luxuriant pine grove that completely conceals the more distant scenery. It is actually nothing more than a background for this garden where no tree or plant other than moss is to be seen, and it appears to have the role of emphasizing the whiteness and coldness of the garden itself. The white expanse of gravel, with its fifteen stones, seems to have sunk deep into the dark green of the pines, as though it were absorbed in meditation, and visitors here can listen, so to speak, to the soliloquy of voiceless Buddhist teachings. It is therefore likely that such visitors, if they are told that this garden was once a shakkei garden, will be astonished. Nevertheless, that is what it appears to have been, at least up to the Taisho era, which began in 1912.

In 1911 the Western-style painter Kinkichiro Honda (1850–1921) published a book entitled *Nihon Meien Zufu* (Paintings of Famous Japanese Gardens). Among the beautiful water colors in the book is a painting of the Ryoan-ji garden, and it is pictured not as merely an enclosed stone garden but as a shakkei garden. Honda notes with surprise that it is based on the same concept as that of the teahouse on the cliff of Takagamine, one of the hills of Kyoto, and that the master gardeners of the past were at one with those of the present in employing this concept, despite the great differences between their time and ours.

Some six decades ago, when Honda pictured the garden in his book, the grove of pines beyond the wall was fairly dense, though not so dense as now. Still, there were a good many trees. Unlike the garden of the Entsu-ji, however, the Ryoan-ji garden is located at the edge of a bluff that lies just beyond the wall, and only the upper halves of the pine trees were visible, just as they are today. In other words, the borrowed scenery could not be viewed through the trunks of trees with high branches. In fact, even then the branches were dense enough to close off the distant view, and for this reason the trees were trimmed, so that through the cleared space one could see an elegant-looking hill, exactly as though it were enclosed in a picture frame. This was Otokoyama, some sixteen kilometers to the south and about 143 meters in height, with the Iwashimizu Hachiman Shrine at its summit. Quite clearly the pine trees played the role of intermediary scenery here, but we can say that the sky also had its role in capturing Otokoyama alive.

One wonders when the concept of this garden took shape. There are people who think that the garden must have been completed in the summer of 1499, when the ridgepole of the abbot's residence at the Ryoan-ji was raised. Naturally, if there had been no large trees growing beyond the edge of the garden at that time, it would have been impossible to capture Otokoyama alive by using their trunks to draw it into the garden. We know, however, that the land here was once the site of a villa owned by the Tokudaiji family and that in 1450 the estate became the property of the shogun's deputy Hosokawa Katsumoto, who later converted it into the Ryoan-ji. It is therefore not unlikely that large pine trees were already growing there beyond the clay wall. Still, according to present-day garden designers, there would have been a way to capture Otokoyama alive even if there had been no trees growing there at all. If the shape of Otokoyama suggests two waves, they tell us, then the fifteen stones in the garden represent fifteen waves, and thus a rhythm of contours would have been established, with the stones playing the role of links to draw the hill into the garden. Although I put no trust at all in this idea, it may just be possible to capture distant scenery alive by such a synchronization of rhythms.

5: TO CAPTURE WITH A WOODS

In the autumn of 794 the emperor Kammu issued an edict ordering that the capital be moved to Heian-kyo, as the city of Kyoto was then called. Eleven centuries later, in 1894, the city submitted a petition to the minister of agriculture and commerce for the opening there of the Fourth National Industrial Exposition in commemoration of the eleven-hundredth anniversary of this event. The city of Osaka also submitted a petition that it be made the site of the exposition, but because of the historical significance of the date it was decided to award the honor to Kyoto and to open the exposition in the spring of 1894. In that year, however, the Sino-Japanese War of 1894–95 broke out, and the exposition was postponed until the hostilities had ended. It was finally opened on April 1, 1895, and ran for four months, ending on July 31.

The exposition site at Okazaki covered an area of 165,500 square meters in which the buildings occupied almost 29,000 square meters. Some 73,000 people submitted a total of about 170,000 items for display, and attendance at the exposition totaled around 1,113,000. In anticipation of transporting this great number of people to the exposition grounds, the Kyoto Electric Railway Company constructed Japan's first municipal electric railway line, which ran from Kyoto Station to Okazaki and was later extended to Kitano. Over this line traveled the streetcars whose bells were to earn them the nickname of *chinchin densha,* or ting-a-ling streetcars. The railway continued for some sixty-six years, making its final run in 1961.

So, in 1895, just over eleven hundred years after the emperor Kammu took part in the congratulatory rites held in the Daigoku-den (Palace Council Hall) to celebrate the establishment of Kyoto as the new capital, the city honored the anniversary with commemorative festivities. The present Heian Shrine, a half-scale copy of the original Daigoku-den in eighth-century Kyoto, was built at this time in accordance with plans drawn by the newly graduated young architect Chuta Ito. The three gardens behind it were planned by the first Jihei Ogawa, the finest among Kyoto's garden designers of the day.

The reason why the city of Kyoto showed a great interest in using its eleven-hundredth anniversary as an occasion for sponsoring the Fourth National Industrial Exposition was that from around 1877 its industries had been suffering a decline brought on by a lack of industrial capital. In 1881, when Governor Kunimichi Kitagaki replaced his predecessor, Governor Makimura, he undertook plans for the construction of a canal leading into Kyoto from Lake Biwa. Construction began in mid-1885 under the supervision of the twenty-three-year-old engineer Sakuro Tanabe, and the canal was completed in March 1890. It had three chief purposes: to supply water for irrigation to the northern part of Kyoto, to serve for the transportation of cargo, and to furnish water power for the famous textile industry of the Nishijin district. In 1891 an electric-power plant was completed, and it became possible to convert water power into electrical power.

At first glance it may appear that this enterprise had no relationship at all with the construction of gardens, but actually there was a close connection between the two. The clear water running plentifully through the canal provided an opportunity to develop the land adjacent to the Nanzen-ji into a site for high-class villas—the area known as Nanzenji Kusakawa-cho. Here, in 1896, on the land where the famous Edo-period restaurant Echigoya once stood, the military and political leader Aritomo Yamagata built his villa Murin-an. In the same year the villa Seifu-so was constructed here, and Seiichi Someya, president of the Kanegafuchi Spinning Company built his Juen-tei, which in his son Kanji's generation became the property of Eikichi Kimura and then, after the Pacific War, was purchased by Konosuke Matsushita and renamed Shinshin-an. Many more villas were built in Nanzenji Kusakawa-cho during the first two decades of the present century, when Japan enjoyed an era of considerable prosperity. And the man who designed the gardens for most of these villas was the same Jihei Ogawa who designed the gardens of the Heian Shrine. His business of garden design, conducted under the professional name of Ueji (a combination of the character for "to plant" and the character *ji* in his first name), grew increasingly prosperous as a result of assignments like these.

Ueji I, as the first-generation Ogawa came to be called, was the foremost garden designer of the Meiji and the Taisho eras. He made a mental compilation of all the design techniques represented in Kyoto gardens of the Edo period, and he was unsurpassed in his skill at using them. Almost all his gardens were stroll gardens arranged around the nucleus of a pond, but they were quite different from the daimyo gardens of Edo. He never undertook to incorporate copies of famous scenic and historic places as the designers of Edo daimyo gardens did. In fact, some of the Tokyo gardeners considered his gardens rather artificial and contrived and gave them the label *sakuteiteki no niwa,* or fabricated gardens.

Aritomo Yamagata, army field marshal and later prime minister, was the incarnation of feudalistic clan government, but he also had a certain amount of discernment about gardens and, in fact, sometimes stepped forward with advice of his own when garden projects were under way, as he did, for example, in the instances of the Chinzan-so garden in Tokyo and the Koki-an garden in Odawara. Therefore it was only to be expected that he would quite forcefully and frequently try to impose his opinions on Jihei Ogawa during the construction of the garden at the Murin-an. Even today in Kyoto people recount the episode in which Ogawa is said to have told the masterful field marshal: "Mr. Yamagata, when it comes to maneuvering armies, you are number one in Japan, but when it comes to making this garden, leave it to me." After that, we are told, Yamagata never meddled with the construction of the garden.

The Nanzenji Kusakawa-cho area adjoins the Higashiyama range of hills, at the foot of which stand such buildings as the temples Nanzen-ji and Eikan-do. The owners of the villas by no means overlooked the distant views from their property, nor, of course, did Ogawa, who adroitly captured the exterior scenery alive for the gardens he built there. For the Murin-an garden (Plates 20–23) he used water from the recently completed canal to create a brook and a shallow pond in the gently sloping terrain. Paths were laid out to make this a stroll garden, and for the borrowed scenery Ogawa captured the Higashiyama range alive. The capturing device was two small forests that stood in the background of the garden, and the layout was so arranged that the hills were viewed through a V-shaped notch between the two stands of trees. The composition here was quite easy to understand, and it typified Ogawa's frequent use of woods to draw borrowed scenery into the garden design.

The garden of the Shinshin-an (Plates 24–27) was designed around the same time as that of the Murin-an. Although the techniques employed in the two gardens are similar, there are certain differences in style. The actual construction of the Shinshin-an garden was supervised by Ogawa's colleagues Tomokichi and Gembei. Since the topography here is more varied than that of the Murin-an, the techniques are somewhat more florid. The north side of the garden is occupied by a grove of cryptomeria trees, and the ground beneath them, apparently once planted with shrubbery, is now partly spread with fine white gravel. On clear days the trunks of the trees seem to float upward in the sunlight, creating a bright and clean effect. Just as it does in the Murin-an garden, water flows in from the canal by way of a stream to form a pond. Regrettably, however, the culverts in the Murin-an garden have been allowed to clog up, and water no longer enters there in plentiful supply. The waterfalls have dwindled to a mere trickle, and the untrimmed shrubbery has the slovenly look of an unshaved beard. For the most part, the original beauty of the garden has been lost. The Shinshin-an garden, on the other hand, is no less beautiful today than it was in the past.

In the Shinshin-an garden, as he did in the garden of the Murin-an, Ogawa used the capturing device of a woods to incorporate part of the Higashiyama scenery into the design. The woods in this case is principally made up of pine trees, and the borrowed scenery includes the hills Yokaku and Dokushu (together known as the Nanzenji Hills) and the Ayato Forest. But the main object of capture is the huge triple gate of the Nanzen-ji itself. This two-story structure, completed in 1628, has a roof of heavy tile and is provided with three entrances in its nine-meter front. In the distance, halfway up the hill to the right from the great gate, there is a bell tower, but in the shakkei view it plays no more than a supporting role to the gate itself. Ogawa captured the gate at the point where the two pine-covered slopes of the intermediary scenery begin their gentle rises to right and left. Today only the upper roof of the gate can be seen from the Shinshin-an garden, but it seems likely that in former times, when the villa was still known as the Juen-tei, the pine trees had not yet grown so tall, and the whole upper structure of the gate could be seen. The upper roof must then have cast a shadow to create the attractive illusion that it was floating in midair. It is probably correct to assume that the bell tower, the two hills, and the Ayato Forest are only accompaniments to the main theme of the Nanzen-ji gate in the borrowed scenery.

Although the pinewoods beyond the lawn and the pond in this garden serve as a device to capture the shakkei view, they also play the role of a trimming line. No doubt there are some people who think it would be better if more of the Nanzen-ji gate could be seen. But it would do no good to go up to the second floor of the villa in order to get a better view of it, for the trimming line was determined on the basis of the ground-level or first-floor view. From the second-floor level one sees unwanted scenery beyond the pine-grove trimming line.

The Isui-en in Nara (Plates 37–39) is also a shakkei garden. In fact, it consists of two gardens: the west garden, built in the 1670's by the textile merchant Kiyosumi Michikiyo, and the so-called rear garden, built in the early 1900's by Tojiro Seki. Kiyosumi was a trader in a popular type of fine-quality ramie cloth made in Nara, and it is interesting to note that the rear garden contains mementos of his trade, for the steppingstones in the pond once served as mortars in preparing the sizing for the ramie cloth of Nara.

The rear garden as we see it today was designed by the gardener Horitoku, who enjoyed the patronage of the Ura Senke school of the tea ceremony. The pavilion called the Hyoshin-tei, which stands to the west of the pond, is the work of the master carpenter Seibei Kimura, another expert frequently employed by the Ura Senke school. For its borrowed scenery, which is meant to be viewed from a point near the Hyoshin-tei, the garden captures the Great South Gate of the Todai-ji and the so-called Three Hills of Nara, and the device that effects the capture is the woods of the Himuro Shrine. It hardly needs to be added that the main object of the shakkei view is the Great South Gate. If there is any fault in the view, it is that the line of the hill Wakakusayama cuts across the roof lines of the gate and thus produces a certain instability in the composition. Before the rear garden was built, it might have been possible to capture a view of the gate from the Sanshu-tei pavilion, the thatch-roofed structure in the west garden, and in this case the gate might have been given a more stable position in the design, with the woods of the Himuro Shrine still serving as the intermediary scenery. Today, however, there is no way of verifying this possibility because of the several structures that now stand in the rear garden.

As an example of a shakkei garden in Edo (the present Tokyo) in which a woods was used to capture distant scenery, the garden of the now vanished villa Toyama-so was no doubt the most imposing. The Toyama-so was built in the 1660's by Tokugawa Mitsutomo, a daimyo of the Owari branch of the Tokugawa clan—the clan that ruled Japan from 1603 to 1868. The vast garden of this villa, measuring some 45,000 square meters in area, was the largest daimyo garden in Edo, and its design motif was a reproduction of the scenery of Odawara, one of the fifty-three post stations on the Tokaido, the famous highway between Edo and Kyoto.

The main structure in the garden was the residence known as the Yokei-do, and it was from here that Mount Fuji was captured alive as the borrowed scenery. The capture was accomplished by means of an intermediary grove of pine trees whose branches were pruned or trained into graceful shapes—a technique often employed by the previously noted garden designer Jihei Ogawa. Because of its shakkei view, the Yokei-do was also known as the Fujimi Goten, or Fuji View Palace. Regrettably, the Toyama-so villa has long since disappeared from the Tokyo scene.

6: TO CAPTURE WITH POSTS AND EAVES

THE JIKO-IN TEMPLE is located in Yamato Koriyama in Nara Prefecture. When one reaches the western foot of the hill on which it stands, he sees no difference between the hillside path and the path leading up any ordinary nameless hill. There is no gate—only the rather broad trail stretching ahead. A careful look, however, reveals a wooden fence at the top of the ascent and, beyond it, what appears to be a residence.

At the top, to the right of the path, there is a gate, and one passes through it to enter a level zigzag walk paved with small flat stones known as *arare koboshi,* or hailstones. The way here becomes somewhat narrower, and it is bordered on both sides by luxuriant shrubbery (Plate 34). One has the illusion of walking through remote mountains and solitary valleys. Even in the daytime this narrow path is dusky, and the view ahead shows nothing but trees and shrubbery. Eventually the path turns to the right, and through the shrubbery one glimpses a thatch-roofed gate. It is a two-story structure of considerable height, and it makes the approach even more dusky. But once one has passed through it, there suddenly appears a bright garden enclosed by a hedge and a building (Plate 2). Visitors to the Jiko-in, on arriving at this point after the long and shadowy approach, are likely to sigh with relief.

The stone-paved walk leads directly to a thatch-roofed building at the right. If one walks straight ahead he arrives at the *genkan,* or guest entrance. A slight turn to the right will bring him to a gate leading into the garden, while a similar turn to the left will bring him to the everyday entrance to the building. It is difficult, however, to believe that this country-style structure is a temple called the Jiko-in.

The temple was founded in 1663 by the low-ranking daimyo Katagiri Sadamasa (1605–73), but visitors unacquainted with this fact might well mistake it for a former hillside villa. Actually it was established as a branch temple of the Daitoku-ji in Kyoto, and it still holds that position today. The reason for its rustic style is that its founder was also the founder of the Sekishu school of the tea ceremony, and elegant rusticity, of course, has always been a distinguishing characteristic of teahouse architecture. Moreover, the concept of Katagiri's shakkei garden is by no means unrelated to the spirit of the tea ceremony, even though, as we have observed earlier, the tea garden itself is never in shakkei style.

Let us enter the Jiko-in as a visitor would, going in by way of the guest entrance. It would do just as well to enter through the everyday door or through the garden gate, since the same effects are anticipated, once one is inside, and there is thus no real difference among the entrances. All of them are small, and since the interior of the building is closed off from the outdoors by means of the sliding translucent panels called *shoji,* we cannot see what lies beyond. Because we do not know what this view is, we are most likely to look forward to it. Or it may be that we see this building as nothing more than an ordinary residence and therefore expect to see nothing special at all.

We are led into the main room and invited to sit down on the tatami mats. Then, when the shoji are opened, we suddenly see before us the vast expanse of the Yamato Plain (Plate 35). In summer, when all the shoji and the interior sliding partitions (*fusuma*) have been removed, one comes upon this imposing view the instant he steps into the room. In either case, the effect is decidedly dramatic.

The concept here is truly admirable. During the long walk over the narrow path leading up from the foot of the hill to the thatch-roofed two-story gate, the visitor is given the illusion of journeying through a secluded mountain valley, and his feeling of tension is somewhat relieved when he reaches the small enclosed garden in front of the temple building and pauses there for breath. Then, after stopping again for a moment at the entrance, he is suddenly overwhelmed by the magnificent view of the Yamato Plain. Interestingly enough, the shakkei concept in this case undoubtedly derives from the design of the tea garden, which, as we have noted, gives careful consideration to the psychological effects of space that the guest experiences as he moves along the steppingstone path from the gate to the teahouse entrance. Like the tea garden, the Jiko-in garden serves as a prologue to the major event, but of course the events in these two instances are totally different. Once the tea-ceremony guest has passed through the low sliding-door entrance to the teahouse, he finds himself in a small secluded world in which the garden has no part, but once the visitor to the Jiko-in has entered the temple, he is introduced to the vast shakkei view of the Yamato Plain that has been incorporated into the garden design. Truly, this is the sort of large-minded garden technique that one would expect of a daimyo who was also a tea master. Nevertheless, it is improper to discuss the borrowed scenery of the Jiko-in garden without reference to the approach by which one reaches it.

The trimming line for the shakkei view is a low hedge that borders the gravel-spread garden on the east side of the building. But the expanse of the Yamato Plain that one sees beyond the hedge is not merely a beautiful view, for it is captured alive by the main building of the Jiko-in itself—specifically by the eaves and two posts of the veranda. In fact, we can compare the capturing device here to the tree trunks that link the view of Mount Hiei to the Entsu-ji garden. But it is the horizontal line of the eaves rather than the posts that plays the more important role in effecting the capture of the Yamato Plain. If the eaves of the Jiko-in veranda were less broad, they would allow too much of the sky to be seen, and thus the view of the plain would degenerate into nothing more than a commonplace sight. As it is, the horizontal lines of the eaves and the hedge form a kind of long picture frame, so that we view the plain as though it were a painting. Because the borrowed landscape here is so large, the east garden is all the more effective for having only a few rocks arranged on its spread of gravel.

Although the view from inside the Jiko-in demonstrates the use of posts and eaves to capture the distant landscape of the Yamato Plain, it should be noted here that the view from the garden itself depends upon a different capturing device. Here the scenery of the plain is drawn into the garden by the trunks of venerable pine trees through which one sees a reservoir and a neighboring village lying beyond the foot of the hill on which the Jiko-in stands (Plate 36).

7: TO CAPTURE WITH THE SKY

In JAPANESE the character for sky is also the character for emptiness. It means both the heavens and the blank spaces that are a distinguishing trait of Oriental painting. In calligraphy, which is in itself a form of painting, it means the spaces in which no characters are written. And in Japan, of course, painting and gardens have long had an intimate relationship.

Early in the Edo period there was introduced into Japan from China a book called *Chieh-tzu Yuan Hua-ch'uan,* which is known in Japanese as *Kaishi-en Gaden* and in English as *The Mustard-Seed Garden Painting Manual.* This book, reprinted in Japan, had a strong influence on Japanese painters. It had its origin when the Ming-dynasty literary-school painter Li Liu-fang (1575–1629) made a compilation of the techniques of painting such subjects as trees, mountains, rocks, human figures, and the like. Li's examples were then classified by Wang An-chieh and published by Li Li-weng in four volumes. Among the subjects presented are sixteen techniques for painting groups of rocks, and these, it is interesting to note, are all surprisingly similar to the techniques for arranging rocks in Japanese gardens. This is not to say, of course, that *The Mustard-Seed Garden Painting Manual* had a direct influence on Japanese gardens, but it testifies to the fact that painting and garden design developed in close relationship with each other. Just as the study of painting in the West begins with techniques of painting the nude, so the study of ink painting in the East begins with techniques of painting rocks. The Chinese book *Chieh-chou Hsueh-hua Lun* (Chieh-chou's Theory of Painting) says: "In order to learn to paint, one must invariably learn how to paint rocks. Of all the techniques of using the brush, none are more difficult than those required for rocks, and no subject calls for a greater range of techniques than rocks do. If one has mastered the painting of rocks, he has acquired the ability to paint all other subjects equally well."

Nevertheless, the relationship between garden design and Oriental painting is by no means limited to the matter of rock arrangements. In Japanese painting, the techniques of composition, the view of nature, and the manner of achieving harmony often contributed, if only in part, to fundamental concepts of garden design. Moreover, there was a time when the painter himself was both a garden designer and a leader in the construction of gardens.

For example, the *Konjaku Monogatari* (Tales of Long Ago), written in the late Heian period, mentions the painter Kudara no Kawanari (782–853), a descendant of a naturalized Korean in Japan, and informs us that he planned the rock arrangements for the garden of the Taki Palace. This is the earliest record of a painter who engaged in garden design.

Toward the end of the ninth century there appeared the painter Kose no Kanaoka, who is said to have been the first artist to put aside the conventional *kara-e* style of painting—that is, painting in the Chinese manner—and to replace it with the native Japanese style known as yamato-e. He is thus regarded as the originator of the yamato-e style. A Momoyama-period (1568–1603) miscellany called the *Shugaisho* tells us that Kanaoka designed the rock-and-pond arrangement of the imperial garden Shinsen-en, and this may very well be true, for another record notes that he was placed in official charge of the garden and its maintenance. Since Heian-period gardens displayed strong yamato-e influence both in composition and in detail, it is quite likely that Kanaoka employed his skill in that style of painting when he supervised the construction of the garden.

Another painter who also designed gardens was Kanaoka's great-grandson Hirotaka. He was active from the late tenth through the early eleventh century and achieved fame as the first artist to bring the yamato-e style to perfection. His professional name is variously written with three different combinations of characters, all of which are read as Hirotaka, and his name as a Buddhist priest was Engen. He attained the rank of senior artist in the official painting bureau (*edokoro*)—that is, he served as a court painter.

In the year 1001 he was one of those who accompanied the retired emperor Kazan on a journey to the Engyo-ji, a temple in Harima Province (now part of Hyogo Prefecture). There he copied a portrait of the Buddhist saint Shoku, putting the finishing touches to this work after he had returned to Kyoto. He is also said to have painted pictures for Fujiwara Yorimichi's celebrated villa at Uji, which survives today as the Phoenix Hall of the Byodo-in. According to Tachibana Toshitsuna's *Treatise on Garden Making,* Hirotaka was a master of garden design who was also well versed in the various taboos of the art: the numerous prohibitions and superstitions that were part of an elaborate code of manners and customs in the Heian age. Toshitsuna quotes him as saying: "One must never arrange rocks carelessly. If one should violate even one taboo, the owner of the garden will inevitably suffer serious consequences, and the prosperity of his house will be brief."

Still another painter who designed gardens was En'en, a contemporary of Hirotaka's. But En'en, unlike Hirotaka and Kanaoka, who were professional painters and garden designers at the same time, was a nonprofessional artist of aristocratic lineage. He was a grandson of the regent Fujiwara Koretada and the third son of the counselor of state Yoshikane, who later entered the Buddhist priesthood. In 986, En'en himself entered the priesthood at Mii-dera and eventually became a master of Esoteric Buddhism. According to the *Eiga Monogatari* (Tales of Glory) and the earlier mentioned *Konjaku Monogatari,* he painted illustrations of the *Kannon Sutra* on the pillars of the Yakushi-do at the Hojo-ji in Kyoto, as well as one hundred representations of the Buddha for the Golden Hall of the same temple. We also learn from these sources that he was known as "zotei no En'en"—that is, the architect En'en—although another record tells us that "architect" here may have been an error for "garden designer." (The Japanese words used in these two cases are homonymous, but their written forms are different.) In any event, it seems not to matter whether En'en was also an architect or not. If we assume that the *Eiga Monogatari* and the *Konjaku Monogatari* are correct, then he must have excelled in architecture as well as in garden design. The *Treatise on Garden Making* states that he transmitted to posterity a record of rock arrangements that had been employed before the *Treatise* itself was written. It also appraises him as a tasteful and elegant painter. En'en died in the early spring of 1040.

Thus in the Heian period, when the fundamental style of the traditional Japanese garden was established, the yamato-e painters played an important role in garden making. This fact in itself is clear evidence of the intimate relationship in Japan between the art of painting and the art of garden design. After the middle of the Heian period—that is, late in the tenth century— semiprofessional priest-gardeners began to appear, and with the opening of the Muromachi period in the early fourteenth century there emerged another group of gardeners: the *kawaramono,* or riverbed people, who were for the most part social outcasts. Neither of these developments, however, meant that the relationship between painting and garden design was in any way weakened. As we have already noted with regard to rock arrangements, it was a relationship that could not be denied, and it was evident in the techniques of the shakkei garden as well.

Indeed, the adoption of compositional concepts from Japanese painting was one of the most fundamental of shakkei methods, and by far the most important of these concepts was that of the empty spaces in a picture. Both garden designers and gardeners viewed these empty spaces as corresponding to the sky over a garden, and it was only natural that they should do so. When a shakkei view is so arranged that it has a mountain at right or left inside the imaginary picture frame of the garden, this composition alone is enough to produce instantly the effect of a typical Japanese landscape painting. There is nothing but empty sky at the left or the right, but the mountain is still captured alive by the sky itself. And there is the sense of a serenely beautiful poem inscribed on the picture, as one often finds on a Japanese ink painting, or of words of praise written on it by an admirer. A cultured observer of the scene will no doubt recall a famous poem of ancient or modern times, or, if he is a person of talent, may very well compose a poem of his own.

But if the mountain occupies the center of the borrowed scenery, the sky is divided in half and therefore probably cannot serve as a capturing device. In a case like this, it will no doubt be necessary to use some such device as large trees placed both behind and in front of the trimming line.

The Upper Garden of the Shugaku-in villa (or, as it is officially called, the Shugaku-in Detached Palace) makes use of a vast stretch of sky to capture its shakkei view (Plates 4, 10–13). The other two gardens of the estate—the Lower Garden and the Middle Garden (Plates 14, 16)—are not of the shakkei type and are considerably less imposing in design than the Upper Garden, to which they constitute the approach. Let us pay a brief visit to the Upper Garden.

We enter by way of the gate called the Onarimon. Before us we see an upward-sloping path with stone steps bordered on both sides by tall hedges. As we ascend the path, we see nothing beyond the walls formed by the hedges, and our destination is not clear. Although the height to which we climb is only some ten meters above the gate, we feel that it is a good deal farther than this from the gate to the top of the hill. To some visitors, no doubt, there is something oppressive about the climb. But the designer of the garden intended to show us nothing at this point except the hedges and the stone steps, so that, when we reach the top and suddenly see the magnificent view spread out before us, we will find it all the more delightful. It was, from the first, a carefully calculated design.

We know, of course, that the Jiko-in garden employs the same kind of plan. Katagiri Sadamasa, who designed the Jiko-in, and the emperor Gomizuno-o, who designed the Shugaku-in villa, were both superlative masters of the art of tea, and it is worthy of special attention that they did not confine themselves to the tea ceremony alone but extended its concepts to include architecture, garden design, and other arts as well.

The teahouse at the top of the hill is the Rin'un-tei (Plate 9), a small pavilion with one six-mat room, one three-mat room, and a board-floored area of somewhat over six square meters. It is surrounded by an earth-floored area under its rather broad eaves. The board-floored section, which forms a kind of veranda, is known as the Senshi-dai, or Poem-washing Platform, and it is said that guests at poetry parties held by the emperor in the Rin'un-tei once sat here to polish their verses as they listened to the sound of the nearby waterfall.

The view from the Rin'un-tei is indeed superb. Directly in front of us the expansive hedge runs downward to the near shore of the Pond of the Bathing Dragon (Plates 12, 13), which is fed by three mountain streams directed into it. The water, like a mirror, reflects the trees and shrubbery along its edges and the great sky above. At the far side of the pond, on the outer slope of the dike that was built to retain the water, is the Great Hedge, which forms the western boundary of the Upper Garden. Beyond the valley at the foot of the Great Hedge, pine-forested hills stand in the middle distance, and above them, in the remote background, we see the summits of Iwakura, Nagatani, Hataeda, Kurama, Kibune, and other hills and mountains rising tier on tier. And then, arching over the whole scene, the immense sky—the sky without which it would be impossible for this vast garden of some 26,500 square meters to capture the mountains to the west and to the north.

Because Shugaku-in is an imperial property and can be visited only by special permission and at designated hours, we are required to see it in the daytime. But in the past it was thought that it showed its greatest beauty at other hours, particularly in the evening. The Middle Garden was formerly part of the temple Rinkyu-ji, whose evening bell, sounding throughout the reaches of the estate, spoke of the essential pathos of things, of "thoughts that do often lie too deep for tears." Behind the forest-covered mountains of Matsugasaki the sun went down, and dusk crept upward from the valleys. In the depths of the night, rain might sound on the roof of the Rin'un-tei, and after the rain the silhouettes of the distant mountains would be ranged against a moonlit sky. At twilight in winter one might look out on a landscape draped with snow. From hour to hour and from season to season the borrowed scenery, like the scenery within the garden itself, altered its appearance and its mood, offering the same infinite variety of aspects that it still offers today. One can say of all Japanese gardens that they seek to bring pleasure through the hourly and seasonal changes in the values and aspects of their scenery, but it is the Shugaku-in garden and its shakkei landscape that are most memorable in this respect.

8: TO CAPTURE WITH A
STONE LANTERN

THE JOJU-IN is the priests' quarters of the famous Kiyomizu Temple (Kiyomizu-dera) in Kyoto. The temple is besieged by countless sightseers, but few of them, after passing through the Niomon—the Gate of the Two Deva Kings—take the leftward path through the grove to visit the Joju-in and the small garden (Plates 28, 29) that lies along the south side of its main room. In his *Tsukiyama Teizoden Kohen* (Constructing Landscape Gardens: Part Two), published in 1716, Ritoken Akisato introduces the Joju-in garden as "a garden of elegance and warmth." I shall probably not be misunderstood if I offer the criticism that it might be more appropriate today to speak of it as a garden of serene clarity. Certainly there is always a fountain of crystal-clear water there in the stone basin donated to the Joju-in in the late sixteenth century by the military dictator Hideyoshi. This large receptacle is of a shape that suggests the hanging sleeves of a woman's kimono.

There are some who say that the garden was designed by Soami, the same artist who is sometimes credited with having designed the Ryoan-ji garden, but of course there is no authority for this attribution. Small though it is, the garden has a pond with a steppingstone path of the tea-garden type around it. There are two stone lanterns: the Dragonfly Lantern on a small island in the center of the pond and the Ball Lantern at the edge of the pond. All this clearly indicates the influence of the tea garden, and therefore we know that the Joju-in garden cannot be traced back as far as the Muromachi period, which antedated the spread of tea-garden influence. One theory says that the garden underwent reconstruction by Kobori Enshu, whom we have already noted as a Kyoto tea master and designer. Another maintains that it was built by the *haiku* and *waka* poet Matsunaga Teitoku (1571–1653).

Regardless of who built it, however, the garden as we see it today must date from around 1629, for it employs a concept typical of the Edo period: its rocks, plants, and other features bear elegant names that are intended to stimulate the viewer's imagination and enhance his pleasure. One rock, for example, is known as the Eboshi Ishi, since it is shaped like an ancient court nobleman's formal hat. A camellia tree carries the name Wabisuke Tsubaki because it belongs to a group of miniature-flowered camellias associated with the celebrated tea master Sen no Rikyu, who once received such a tree from the merchant Wabisuke of Sakai. The garden is bounded on its south and west sides by a low hedge.

There is another small garden to the west of the main room: a rather casual garden that looks as though it had been constructed to make use of the vacant space at the edge of the premises. It contains only a single large evergreen oak with a triangular stone lantern under it and, at the edge of the veranda, a water basin of natural stone. Beyond the hedge that forms the boundary of the garden is a valley of maple trees. Farther below, the houses of the Shimogyo section of Kyoto line the streets, and in the more remote distance one sees Arashiyama and Atagoyama. A layman might think that what the Joju-in garden should capture is this scenery lying to the west of it, but the designer of the garden thought differently.

Just outside the south garden is the dale called Yuyadani, and beyond it, adjacent to Otowayama, rises a gently sloping hill with no distinctive features and no special elegance. Behind it a small part of the hill Kodaijiyama can be seen. Observing this view, we cannot help wondering if it would not have been more effective to capture the view from the west garden: the valley of maples that turn scarlet in autumn, the houses lining the streets below, and the hills standing in the distance. But it is more comfortable for the main room of the building to face the south, particularly in winter, and if it faced the west, the afternoon heat in summer would be unbearable. For this reason the main garden had to be constructed on the south side.

The hill adjoining Otowayama is a nameless, ordinary hill. It is not beautiful like Mount Hiei or elegant like Arashiyama. How did the designer capture this nameless hill alive? We are surprised at the ingenuity of his technique. He has placed a stone lantern in a small clearing on the side of the hill— an irresistibly clever idea (Plate 29). For the very reason that the hill is commonplace, the lantern stands out to all the greater advantage in its role of accomplishing the capture. Again, because the hill is so ordinary, the south garden itself has a large number of rocks and trees and a pond with a complicated shoreline—all for the purpose of creating a balance. Without this contrast between simplicity and complexity, both the garden and its shakkei view would have lost their interest. In any case, the garden has been given greater depth through the incorporation of borrowed scenery that would otherwise have been nothing more than an unintegrated background. In an instant, so to speak, the small space of the garden is expanded through the magic of the stone lantern that captures the hill. Perhaps this is a kind of psychological trick, but its effectiveness certainly cannot be denied.

Gardeners of the Edo period frequently used stone lanterns as capturing devices, just as their present-day counterparts do. Let us suppose that beyond a low hedge marking the boundary of a garden there is a beautiful landscape or perhaps the extensive garden of a neighboring residence. As it stands, it is nothing more than an attractive view. But if the hedge is arranged in two staggered sections, with a low wooden gate at the point where one section ends and the other begins, and then a stone lantern is placed immediately behind the hedge, one creates the illusion that the landscape or the neighboring garden belongs to the garden in the foreground. This is quite obviously a trick.

Stone votive lanterns were originally used by temples and shrines alone, but the tea masters of the sixteenth century assigned them the new role of providing nighttime illumination in their tea gardens, and eventually they came to serve as decorative elements in residential gardens. Then, assuming still another role, they were put to use as devices for integrating borrowed scenery with the garden itself.

9: TO CAPTURE WITH A WINDOW

Matsudaira sadanobu (1758–1829), daimyo of Shirakawa and initiator of shogunate economic reforms in the late 1700's, was also a man of letters who had a fondness for garden design. In his Shirakawa fief was the garden Nanko (South Lake), which was open to the public, and within the compound of his castle there were four gardens. His properties in Edo included the Shogetsu-sai in Fukagawa and the Rikuen-kan in Otsuka. During the Bunka era (1804–17) he built the Yokuon-en garden in the Tsukiji district of Edo. Within this garden stood the villa Meigetsu-ro, on the west side of whose main guest room was a tokonoma (decorative alcove) with a window that captured a view of Mount Fuji. Traditionally, of course, the rear wall of the tokonoma has no opening and is occupied by a hanging scroll. To be sure, it was a rather vulgar taste that would replace the scroll with a window through which one could admire Fuji, to say nothing of the exaggeration of technique that was displayed here, but even this was a device for capturing scenery alive.

Maeda Toshitsune (1593–1658), daimyo of Kaga, had a residence in Otsu, not far from Kyoto. One day Kobori Enshu, after having viewed the garden, criticized it by saying: "The whole arrangement here is too small for the enjoyment of a daimyo. Can't something be done so that those big mountains and the lake can be seen?" Toshitsune thereupon ordered the removal of the artificial hill and the pond from his garden, had one wall of his main guest room opened to form a large window, and thus brought in a view of Mount Hiei, Karasaki on the shore of Lake Biwa, and Mount Mikami. In a word, he succeeded in capturing distant scenery alive by means of a window.

In the several ways we have noted in this chapter and the preceding ones, the majority of gardens had the potentiality of becoming *shakkei* gardens and were able to capture the distant scenery with a variety of devices. By contrast, the *tsuboniwa*, or enclosed garden, which is epitomized by the tea garden, rejected borrowed scenery and turned inward upon itself—or rather, in most cases, found it impossible to use such scenery because of its own limitations of space and exterior environment. Originally both the *tsuboniwa* of the town house and the garden surrounding the teahouse were spaces spontaneously generated between structures built on small sites, and it was therefore impossible for them to borrow scenery outside their boundaries, even if their designers had wanted them to do so. Naturally we cannot ignore these circumstances of their origin, but there is a much more important reason for the absence of borrowed scenery. We must not forget that the great majority of *tsuboniwa* were influenced by the philosophy of the tea ceremony. The tea garden, unlike the usual residential garden, is not meant to be looked at from indoors but to serve as a kind of stage for the teahouse and the tea ceremony itself. Consequently, exterior scenery viewed from the tearoom serves only to distract the guests and prevent them from concentrating on the ceremony. It was required of the tea garden that it be quietly sequestered, as though it were sunk in the depths of a forest.

The warriors of the Momoyama period, at the same time that they busied themselves with erecting gorgeous and gaudy castles and urban mansions, found the leisure to engross themselves in the world of the tearoom and to seek in it those almost indefinable qualities of *wabi* and *sabi,* which we may briefly define here as rustic simplicity and the flavor or patina of age. In the same manner the Japanese garden now developed in two different directions and produced two different but coexisting forms. After the beginning of the seventeenth century, while *shakkei* gardens like those of the Hataeda and Shugaku-in villas, the Joju-in, the Jiko-in, and the abbot's residence at the Daitoku-ji achieved a certain popularity, the *tsuboniwa*—that is, the courtyard garden—came to be increasingly favored among the townspeople. Although they were opposites in character and appearance, the two forms of garden were simply two facets of a single culture.

10: THE BIRTH OF THE COURTYARD GARDEN

In the yamanoue sojiki, an early and important book about the tea ceremony published in 1589, there is the floor plan of a house once owned by the famous tea master Takeno Jo-o (1502–55). The building was a small one that consisted principally of two 4.5-mat guest rooms and a tearoom of the same size. Essentially, it was a teahouse, and what interests us most about it is the tearoom itself. On the south side of the room was a tokonoma about 1.8 meters wide and about 70 centimeters deep. Its framework was of lacquered chestnut wood, and its ceiling, some 21 centimeters lower than of the room itself, was a single wide board of cryptomeria. To the east of the tearoom was a 1.5-mat pantry, partitioned off by sliding fusuma panels. To the north was a slat-floored veranda of about 2.7 meters in length and 91 centimeters in width and, beyond it, a courtyard garden—in those times called a *tsubo-nouchi*—measuring some 2.7 meters by 1.2 meters and known as the *omote no tsubonouchi,* or front courtyard garden. No doubt there were shoji between the veranda and the tearoom. On the west side of the tearoom was another courtyard garden, this one measuring roughly 3.64 by 1.36 meters and called the *waki no tsubonouchi,* or side courtyard garden.

According to another plan of the teahouse, in this case drawn by Takeno Jo-o's pupil Ikenaga Sosaku, the front courtyard garden was known simply as the "garden," while the one at the side was called the *uchi roji* (inner tea garden). From this we can gather that tea-ceremony guests entered the tearoom by way of the side courtyard garden. We can also gather that this tearoom, unlike those in teahouses of the hermitage, or thatched-cottage, style, was of rather open construction, so that the guests, while enjoying the tea ritual, could look out over the veranda at the small garden. Since we are told that pine trees, both large and small, could be seen beyond the wall that enclosed the garden, we can imagine that there was the additional pleasure of listening to the murmur of their boughs on a windy day.

We also find in the above-noted *Yamanoue Sojiki* the plan of a three-mat tearoom of the type used by the most orthodox masters of the tea ceremony: those who adhered to the strictest simplicity and kept the tea paraphernalia to a bare minimum. But even this extremely small tearoom had a courtyard garden of about 2.7 by 1.5 meters in area. A wall somewhat less than a meter in length occupied part of the long side of the tearoom, but the remainder of this side was open to the garden. Four other tearooms are illustrated in addition to the ones already mentioned here, and each had a courtyard garden about 1.8 meters square.

Before the establishment of the teahouse in hermitage style, the ceremonial tearoom had three major features: the tea-serving area (that is, the interior of the room itself), which was open on one side; the adjoining veranda, where the guests sat during the intermission in the tea ceremony and where samurai guests left their swords on a special rack (since the sword was alien to the spirit of the tearoom); and the small courtyard garden, or tsubonouchi, beyond the veranda. Under these conditions, in which the outdoor scenery was in view during the tea ceremony, what the tea masters required as the basis of design for the courtyard garden was that it should not distract the attention of the guests. According to the *Chasho Senrin,* an early tea-ceremony classic, "a garden of this type should preferably have no trees, no shrubs, no ornamental stones, and no ground cover of sand or pebbles, so that the guests will not be distracted by it but can, instead, concentrate on the spirit of tea and on the famous tea bowls and other prized objects that are used." Another classic of the tea ceremony, the *Cha-no-yu Hisho,* informs us that the tearoom of the Sokyo-in at Nara had a few stones arranged at the edge of its veranda but that these did not particularly distract the attention. The courtyard garden of the tea master Murata Juko (1423–1502) had nothing but a single willow tree, and in the garden constructed by Matsuya Hisayoshi (?–1633) according to plans drawn by Karubeya Dosetsu, there were only a ritual water basin and a single maple tree in addition to the steppingstones laid in a ground cover of moss.

These courtyard gardens, which played the role of the earliest tea gardens, were extremely small, and none of them exceeded two *tsubo* (6.62 square meters) in area. If we judge by the examples already noted, we might assume that such gardens originated as early forms of the tea garden, but this is not the case. Before the tea ceremony ever became popular among the common people in cities and towns of the Muromachi period, the courtyard garden had existed as a feature of urban houses. Naturally, such gardens had no relation to the tea garden. We have evidence of this in a decorative screen called *Scenes in and Around Kyoto,* one of a genre of screens that bear the same name and date chiefly from the late Muromachi and the Momoyama periods. This screen, presumably completed in the early sixteenth century and now owned by the Machida family of Tokyo, pictures a number of courtyard gardens, all of which have the same form.

The houses that appear on the screen invariably have their entrances on the side parallel to the ridge of the roof, rather than on the gable end, and each has an earth-floored passage that runs from front to rear. In this respect they are basically the same as the houses of present-day Kyoto. To judge by their size, we can assume that there were usually two rooms or, at most, three. At the front, adjoining the entranceway, were lattices of thick wooden bars, and the entrance was furnished with a door that swung on pivots as well as with a divided curtain of hemp cloth or straw matting. The exit to the back yard was of the same type.

The tsubonouchi, or courtyard garden, was an extension of the back room of the house. Normally, in an urban house, the opening in the back room was a latticed window, but when there was a courtyard garden, it was a full opening, and we can safely assume that it was furnished either with a wooden door or with shoji. The garden was enclosed by clay walls roofed with thatch, and one wall had a small latticed window.

It is interesting to note what the above-mentioned Ikenaga Sosaku has to say about walls of this type. "For enclosing a tea garden," he writes, "clay walls are best, and if small stones of proper size are embedded in them, they become all the more attractive when they are sprinkled with fresh water." Sosaku's remarks are full of interesting suggestions regarding the characteristics of the courtyard garden as an early form of the tea garden, but we must remember that the courtyard garden was not originally designed to serve the purposes of the tea ceremony.

When the urban commoner's house eventually assumed an open type of front and rear structure, the enclosure that came to be known as the tsubonouchi was required as a kind of shield to protect the privacy of the family. At the same time it offered the advantage of providing space for constructing a small garden. It follows, then, that the tsubonouchi was a necessary adjunct to the early tearoom, which also had a wide opening. And the walls of the tsubonouchi, like those of traditional houses that we see in present-day Kyoto and the surrounding area, were of clay. Also, if it is true that people enjoyed the sight of freshly wet small stones embedded in the walls, it will be safe to assume that these walls were never of white plaster but always of warm-toned and unpretentious earth.

Although it might seem simple enough to provide a house with wide openings, it was no simple matter for the commoners of the Muromachi period to do so. For a house to assume an open structure required the addition of such fittings as shoji and wooden doors, but in those days, when the ordinary carpenter's plane and other sophisticated tools were still un-unknown in Japan, such fittings were exorbitantly expensive. Thus, even though urban houses had vacant areas behind them, only a very small number of people could afford to open the back of the house and build a veranda there. Usually the tsubonouchi was enclosed by walls in which there were no openings except a small window placed high in the one at the rear. Thus even the room facing the broad back yard was dark in the daytime and poorly ventilated. What one saw from the small window of the tsubonouchi was an open space surrounded by the neighboring houses: an area that contained a communal well and a communal toilet and served as a place for children to play and for housewives to dry their laundry.

We take it for granted that the tearoom is floored with tatami, but it was not until the fifteenth and sixteenth centuries, just slightly earlier than the advent of the tearoom, that the common people of Kyoto, Nara, and Sakai used tatami at all in their houses. The tatami-floored room came to be known as a *zashiki,* and a small-sized room with tatami, called a *kozashiki,* served the purpose of a tearoom until the ceremonial tearoom assumed a fixed form.

It was probably in the thirteenth and fourteenth centuries that people began to use tatami in the same way that seating cushions (*zabuton*) are used today—that is, by putting them down when they were needed and taking them up again afterward and storing them in a corner of the room. The reason, of course, was that tatami were too expensive for entire floors to be covered with them. We learn, for example, that in 1397 the Rin'ami house at the Uematsu Manor in the western outskirts of Kyoto was supplied with ten tatami. From what we know today about the use of tatami in commoners' houses of the medieval period, we can place this among the earliest examples of their appearance in such surroundings. In any event, it is important to remember that not only tatami-floored rooms but also the tearoom and the courtyard garden were quite new and fashionable—indeed, "modern"—during the closing years of the Muromachi period and were by no means survivals from the musty past.

An official record of 1572 informs us that the residence of the wealthy merchant Hachiya Josa (1519–71) in the suburbs of Nara had a frontage of almost 30 meters. It is of interest to note that when this residence was given to the Noh actor Taizo under the third Tokugawa shogun, Iemitsu, who ruled from 1623 to 1651, it was recorded as having an area of 1,324 square meters. Among the residences listed in the above-noted record of 1572, it was the largest, and its considerable size can be attributed to two factors: the affluence of its owner Josa and its location on the outskirts of Nara, where land was available for such large-scale construction.

It might seem natural to assume that if the entire property was surrounded by walls, there would be no need to construct a tsubonouchi in front of a room that was open to the outside. In most cases, however, quite the opposite was true, for the premises included not only the quarters of the main family but also those of relatives (families of sons and daughters, for example) and nonrelatives who served as employees of the ménage. According to a record of 1487, for instance, a single residence was made up of a number of conjoined structures, and the largest such residence had no fewer than seven components.

At this time, when the property-owning commoner class was organized by trades and occupations, it copied the system of succession followed by the warrior class and passed on the family headship to the eldest son, who then occupied the main quarters while his aged parents resided in a retreat, or retirement quarters, on the same premises. Therefore when a residence consisted of a number of households of both relatives and nonrelatives living together, a walled enclosure like the tsubonouchi was still necessary to insure privacy.

In any event, as the residences of the urban propertied class took form during this period, it was completely natural that the tsubonouchi, which had come into existence as an indispensable architectural feature, should be made to serve as a garden adjoining the early tearoom. This is not so say, however, that the tsubonouchi was newly and specifically devised for the sake of the tearoom, for it was still the same tsubonouchi as before. At the same time we must remember that, unlike the tea garden of later times, it was meant to be looked at from the tearoom. In this respect it did not differ from the gardens of shoguns and aristocrats of the age, but in spite of its small size it graphically displayed an unconventional attitude toward design. We can observe one example of this unconventionality in the fact that only a single willow tree or a single maple was often planted in the tsubonouchi—a clear violation of a contemporary taboo. During the Higashiyama age, which takes its name from the district of Kyoto where the shogun Ashikaga Yoshimasa (1435–90) lived in his villa the Silver Pavilion and sponsored the elegant Higashiyama culture of ink painting, the Noh drama, the tea ceremony, the Zen-style landscape garden, and the like, it was considered an invitation to misfortune to plant a single tree in a small enclosed garden. The reason for this superstition was simple: the character for "trouble" in Japanese is a single tree inside a boxlike enclosure—that is, 困. In 1466, when Yoshimasa visited the Unjo-in subtemple of the Shokoku-ji, he noted that only a single plum tree was growing in the garden to the west of the temple gate and thereupon pointed out that such an arrangement was taboo in garden design because of its resemblance to the inauspicious ideogram. He then suggested that one or two additional plum trees be planted in the garden.

But it was not merely to keep the tea garden from being distractive that the tea masters planted only one tree there. What is of greater importance is that they set aside conventions in order to pursue their own new aesthetic concepts. Their positive attitude toward design enabled them to create from the commonplace tsubonouchi the unique tea garden of a later age and thereby to extend their influence not only to the gardens of residences in the aristocratic shoin style but also to the courtyard gardens of urban commoners.

11: HIDDEN RETREATS IN THE CITY

L ATE IN 1591, as he tells us in his journal, the lacquerer and art connoisseur Matsuya Hisayoshi went to visit the home of the merchant Okaya Doka in the Higashi Jodo district of Nara. It was only a walk of some fifteen minutes, Hisayoshi says, and because the time was about four o'clock in the morning, long before daybreak, the light was still burning in the lantern in Doka's tea garden. It is this last bit of information—the existence of the tea garden—that specifically interests us here.

Doka had the popular name of Hikojiro, and since he is said to have dealt in gunpowder and lead, we can identify him as a purveyor of military stores. Like many other merchants of his day, he was also a tea master, a virtuous man who was on good terms with the common people of Nara and with those of Kyoto and Osaka as well. He owned a number of prized tea-ceremony objects, among them a much-admired ceramic tea canister, a tea bowl of the ware known as Ise *temmoku,* a Shigaraki water jar, and a specimen of calligraphy by a famous Buddhist priest.

The frontage of the lot on which Doka's house stood was only about 3.18 meters: the same, in fact, as the frontage of ordinary lots in that district of Nara today. We do not know the depth, but if we assume it to have been between 54 and 55 meters at the smallest, then the total area was no more than 174 square meters. The house fronted on an east-west street and faced the north. If we judge by what we know of the street plan of Nara in those days, it was normal for houses to face east or west, and it would be safe to conclude that the building lots were not very deep. On the other hand, if the site was L-shaped, the rear entrance may have been either to the east or to the west. Still, no matter how large we may estimate Doka's place to have been, it is unlikely that it exceeded 100 tsubo, or 331 square meters, in total area.

We know that the frontage of Doka's house was somewhat less than three meters. If we assume that an earth-floored area ran along one side of the interior, as was the case in most houses of the day, the rooms could only have been placed in a row from front to back. We do not know the depth of the house, but we learn that the entrance was on the side rather than on the end that faced the street, and for this reason we can surmise that there were only a few rooms—probably two or three.

In the courtyard behind the house was a tearoom, but we are not told whether it was a separate structure connected to the main building by means of a veranda-corridor or whether it was an extension of the main building. On lots of this width, when houses are crowded together as they are today, one can have at most a courtyard garden and an open area or a garden at the rear. But since Matsuya Hisayoshi's journal tells us that Doka's house had a tea garden with a lantern in it, it is reasonable to think that the houses in the district were not so closely packed as at present. Again, if guests at Doka's house did not pass through the house itself to reach the tearoom, then they must have approached it by way of a narrow passage that lay between the house and the neighboring one. The house to the west of Doka's was that of Daikokuya Akikiyo. It stood on a corner lot with a frontage of 15.6 meters. The house to the east, on a lot whose frontage was 6.06 meters, belonged to Hirakiya Jinzaburo.

In late-sixteenth-century Nara, a building lot like Doka's, with a frontage of only 3.18 meters, was among the narrowest of those owned by commoners whose residences could still include a tearoom. Whether it was for this reason or another, we do not know, but it seems that Doka later moved to the nearby district of Tsubai-cho.

It will be interesting here to make a few comparisons. As we have previously noted, the residence of the Nara merchant Hachiya Josa had a frontage of about 30 meters. Since the total area of his property was around 400 tsubo, or 1,324 square meters, it was roughly the same as that of the present-day Mushanokoji Senke school of tea in Kyoto. Of the other schools of tea in Kyoto that are of comparable size, the Omote Senke occupies an area of about 1,754 square meters and the Yabunouchi about 1,655 square meters. At the Ura Senke, however, the Konnichi-an tearoom and its garden alone take up some 1,701 square meters or about one-fourth of the total area of the establishment. In any case, even though an urban property in the late sixteenth century may have been considered large, it was nevertheless small by modern standards.

Josa's residence on the outskirts of Nara, in addition to the house itself, included a tearoom (*chashitsu*), a pavilion (*chaya*) for such entertainments as poetry parties as well as for the drinking of tea, and a well whose curb was made of discarded whetstones. A small stream flowed behind the property, and the neighboring houses on both sides were one-family residences.

We may take note here of one more residence in the Higashi Jodo district of Nara, where Doka lived: that of Daito Zenshiro, whose lot had a frontage of about 11.66 meters and (we may estimate) an area of between 200 and 300 tsubo—that is, between 662 and 993 square meters. It can be assumed that a lot of this size provided sufficient space for a tea garden along the side of the house, if the owner wished to construct it in this fashion.

In the autumn of 1526 the poet Socho paid a visit to the tea master Murata Soju at his home in Shijo in the Shimogyo section of Kyoto. Soju was the son and successor of Juko, founder of the tea ceremony, and at this time had finally begun to achieve fame in his own right, particularly as the originator of a distinctive style of teahouse. The record that tells of Socho's visit includes several interesting details concerning Soju's garden. As one entered the gate, it says, he saw large pine and cryptomeria trees. Inside the garden, all was clear and tranquil, and several fallen leaves of dark-green ivy, perhaps five or six, lay on the ground.

Three years later, when the nobleman Yamashina Tokitsugu visited Soju, he wrote in his diary: "The teahouse has the look of a small dwelling in the mountains. It expresses great feeling and must truly be called a quiet retreat in the city." In a word, it appears that the scenery of the garden suggested that of a remote place in the mountains. If we look for small present-day gardens in Kyoto that evoke a similar feeling, no doubt the best are those of the Yabunouchi school of tea in Shimogyo-ku (Plates 68–70) and the Hyo-tei (Gourd Pavilion) restaurant in Nanzenji Kusakawa-cho (Plates 71–74).

To return for a moment to the residences of merchants in Nara in the late sixteenth century, we may mention those of the dyer Yajiro in the Muendo district, with a frontage of 6.36 meters; of the tatami dealer Zenshiro (who was a purveyor to the great temple Kofuku-ji) in the same district, with a frontage of 3.39 meters; and of the cosmetics dealer Gengoro (who later became a chief elder in the local government) in Higashi Jodo and the merchant Shinjiro in Wakido, both of which had a frontage of 4.24 meters.

Although there is some variation in these frontages, we may take the average area of the lots to have been around 100 tsubo, or 331 square meters. Today, once a house and a storehouse have been built on a lot of this size, there is absolutely no space left for a tea garden. But in the time of these merchants, houses were not so large as they are at present, and thus at the residence of the merchant Doka there was probably room for a tea garden, as Hisayoshi states in his journal. But Hisayoshi speaks of the tea garden as a roji, and if we are to take this term in its literal meaning of path, it may be that the "garden" was no more than the narrow passage that lay alongside the house and that only a few appurtenances (like the lantern that Hisayoshi mentions) were added to suggest a genuine tea garden.

It was after the Keicho era (1596–1615) that urban houses began to grow larger and more closely crowded together. Books like the *Atago Miyage* (Souvenir of Atago) and the collection of proverbs called *Nara Sarashi Kokon Rigenshu,* both published in 1699, inform us that this era marked the dividing line between the age when houses were comparatively small and the age when they increased in height and area and thus drew closer together.

As for the tearoom itself, its veranda disappeared and was replaced by an earth-floored area under the eaves, while the shoji that filled the side open to the courtyard were supplanted by a wall with a low sliding-door entrance: the previously noted nijiri-guchi. The courtyard garden, no longer meant to be viewed from the tearoom, lost its earlier function, and the former narrow passage known as the roji was transformed into the tea garden (Plates 3, 5, 51–74, 103). Indeed, this roji, once no more than a kind of alleyway, now came to simulate the approach to a mountain retreat in wabi style: the style of elegant rusticity. In what was formerly a space essentially lacking in scenery, a scenic setting was created, and in the once pathless area that constituted the approach to the tearoom (or the teahouse) a path appeared. The open spaces inevitably generated among the closely built urban houses, while still performing the functions of lighting and ventilation, were sublimated into gardens that took on an air of solitary rural beauty: the perfection of the wabi ideal. The natural beauty that had gradually been lost to urbanization was now at least partially restored through the art of the tea ceremony, which brought it back in the form of rustic garden landscapes.

In the Noh-play comic interlude *Shuron* (Arguing About Religion), two Buddhist priests meet on the way to Kyoto and decide to travel together. What is of interest here is not the plot of the story but the fact that the word used for "way" is roji, in this sense carrying an abstract rather than a concrete connotation. In other words, it does not mean a specific road or path but is simply the "way" of "on the way." This was its earlier meaning in Japanese, and it is safe to assume that even in the days of the tea masters Soju and Jo-o, before the tearoom in hermitage (thatched cottage) style was born, the roji in this sense existed. The disappearance of the walls of the tsubonouchi during the time of Juko and Jo-o can be considered to have a connection with the change in the role of the tea garden, which was now no longer to be viewed from the tearoom.

The great difference between the tsubonouchi and the roji was that the former was an enclosed garden designed to be viewed from the tearoom, while the latter was meant to serve as an approach to the tearoom (or tea-house). In other words, the tsubonouchi gave importance to a tranquil scenic or spatial composition to be viewed from a static position, while the roji, designed for carrying out an essential preliminary ritual of the tea ceremony, laid major stress on providing the guests with a series of spatial experiences as they walked through it. To put this even more simply, the tsubonouchi functioned on the premise that the guests would be sitting still, the roji on the premise that they would be in motion. Indeed, one of the most important aspects of the roji is the careful and deliberate attention with which it is designed to produce psychological changes in the people who walk through it.

The tea garden is quite naturally small in scale. Nevertheless, we must give it a position of great importance in the history of the Japanese garden, for it conquered the medieval religious concept of garden design and, finding support in a new aesthetic philosophy, taught a new concept of design that relied on a sequence of spatial experiences to create its own special effects.

12: THREE FORMS OF THE COURTYARD GARDEN

W HEN WE LOOK at the courtyard gardens of traditional-style houses in the Kyoto-Osaka district—particularly those of urban houses in Kyoto and Nara—we discover that almost all of them are patterned after the tea garden. Some are front gardens (Plates 90, 99, 102), some are gardens surrounded by component elements of the house (Plates 92, 100), and some are rear gardens (Plate 96). The smallest of them have an area of only 3 to 4 tsubo (about 10 to 13 square meters), but even the largest do not run to more than 50 tsubo (slightly over 165 square meters). The garden of the Kiichiro Zenta family in Kyoto (Plates 91, 92) is among the largest of the type. As the garden of a residence in *shoin* style—the style traditionally employed for the mansions of daimyo and samurai—it is meant to be viewed from the guest room. At the same time, however, it is a tea garden, for it has a waiting booth for guests, a path laid out with steppingstones, a ritual water basin, and a teahouse. In brief, it copies the form of the classical tea garden.

The usual courtyard garden, on the other hand, is simply a small open area between buildings, and its aesthetic function is combined with those of lighting and ventilation. Even if the house has a tearoom, the courtyard garden does not constitute the approach to the nijiri-guchi entrance. Again, even if the garden has a ritual water basin, the basin is not used for washing the hands and rinsing the mouth in preparation for the tea ceremony. Like the steppingstones and the lantern that may also appear there, it is nothing more than a decorative feature. For these reasons, I prefer to speak of this style of courtyard garden as a tea-garden type and not as a tea garden per se. Still, as one can quite readily see, the model for the urban courtyard garden is the tea garden.

If we stop to think about it, we realize that the courtyard garden in Kyoto and Nara has a long tradition dating back to ancient times. The gardens of Shinto shrines, the enclosed gardens of residences in the *shinden* style (the style employed for imperial palaces and noblemen's mansions in earlier days), the front and rear gardens of priests' quarters and subtemples in the compounds of Buddhist temples—all these are examples of small gardens that display a surpassing concept of design. Why, then, did the city dwellers choose as their sole model the garden created by the tea masters of the sixteenth century? Why did they not construct courtyard gardens in other styles? In their houses they employed gables of the same type as those in temples, shrines, and imperial-palace buildings, but they used a different name for them, and we may therefore ask if it was fear of offending their superiors that prevented them from copying any but the tea-garden style. Still, this does not appear to be an adequate reason for their choice, since tea gardens are also found at temples and shrines, and gardens displaying the tea-garden influence can be found at the same places and at the Kyoto Imperial Palace as well.

At the Kasuga Shrine in Nara a garden spread with fine white gravel lies in the enclosure formed by the entrance hall of the inner sanctuary, the banquet hall, and the connecting corridors. Sometimes the shrine maidens, in their long scarlet skirts, perform dances for the gods in this garden as well as in the dancing hall, where such rituals are ordinarily carried out. It is a bright and tranquil place. Because it is occupied by a single aged apple tree, it has come to be known as the Apple Tree Garden.

The whiteness of the gravel symbolizes the perfect purity that Shinto embodies as one of its ideals (Plate 42). At the same time, it suggests the primitive form of the Japanese garden before it was influenced by Taoism and Buddhism. Other forms of the Shinto garden can be seen at the inner sanctuary of the Ise Shrine, where natural rocks are placed on the gravel-spread ground to symbolize gods, and at the Omiwa Shrine in Nara Prefecture—particularly the gardens of the upper and lower sanctuaries on Mount Miwa. In the ages when the practice of magic controlled all aspects of life, rocks and trees had a profound religious symbolism, and the faultless white of fine white gravel expressed the innocence of the unsullied human heart. The scenery of the Shinto garden was always placid and luminous.

In primitive times, when the Shinto concept of shunning all impurity dominated the life of the Japanese, it was only natural that both the emperor, who was regarded as a divine being, and the local chieftains, who served also as priests, should choose to have white-gravel gardens in front of their palaces, which invariably faced the south. But the age when gods and men were equals and resided in the same buildings gradually gave way to an age in which gods were separated from men. This new age corresponds to the time when the emperor Sujun (reigned 97–30 B.C.) removed the sacred Shinto mirror Yata no Kagami from the imperial palace and enshrined it in Kasanui-mura in Yamato Province (the Nara Prefecture of today), entrusting it there to one of his daughters who was a high priestess.

In the past, the south garden of the imperial palace, whether in Nara or Kyoto or one of the earlier capitals, continued to be a garden of white gravel and was used as the locale for court ceremonies and other events. Here performances of music and dance from China and Korea were given, contests of equestrian archery were held, and foreign envoys were entertained at banquets. It was also the site of poetry parties and garden fetes.

If the south garden was a garden of formality, then the gardens enclosed by the east and west wings of the palace and by the apartments of the court ladies—the true courtyard gardens—were private and far less formal places (Plate 40). Compared with the south garden, on which the shinden-style buildings fronted, the courtyard gardens played a supporting role. Although they were no more than informal settings within the palace compound, it was their very informality that made it quite easy for them to reflect individual tastes. And since they were not dominated by tradition and rigid custom, they contained the essentials for their own development.

In the *Gempei Seisuiki,* a fourteenth-century military romance that deals with the fortunes of the Minamoto and the Taira clans in the civil war that brought the Heian period to a close, there is a description of the Taira leader Kiyomori's *yomogi ga tsubo* (artemisia garden) at his Nishi Hachijo Palace in Kyoto. It seems that Kiyomori was exceedingly fond of the yomogi and, as the *Gempei Seisuiki* relates, ordered the construction of a courtyard garden to be planted with it. He had such an affection for the garden that he spent much time looking at it, both morning and evening, and never once showed any sign of being bored with it, the story says. It is interesting indeed that what found its way into Kiyomori's heart was this courtyard garden, which, as gardens go, was probably the least prominent one at his palace. The yomogi is nothing more than a weed, but when it was planted in the white-gravel garden, the whole setting somehow acquired a look of elegance.

When we visit the Kyoto Imperial Palace today, we see among its gardens a *hagi tsubo,* or courtyard garden of bush clover: an expanse of fine white gravel dotted here and there with clumps of this unassuming plant (Plate 40). There is nothing else there, but the garden has an extremely refined air and a peculiar charm of its own. Again, at the Kyoto temple Ninna-ji, the courtyard garden between the Shinden and the Black Shoin displays a still different aspect of elegance. Here the ground cover is moss instead of white gravel, and clumps of *sasa* (bamboo grass) are planted at irregular intervals on this dark-green carpet (Plate 41).

When we come to think about it, we wonder why the townsmen of the Momoyama and Edo periods did not use gardens like these as models for their own courtyard gardens. In the Edo period, for instance, even though it may have been difficult for the ordinary populace to see such gardens in actuality, they were illustrated in great numbers in Ritoken Akisato's *Tsukiyama Teizoden* (Constructing Landscape Gardens), the first part of a work that has been cited earlier in this book. For this reason, it seems unlikely that the townspeople knew nothing about bright and serene courtyard gardens like those of palaces, temples, and shrines. Moreover, since the enclosed gardens of the crowded urban districts tended to be rather dark and gloomy, it would seem only logical that the much brighter courtyard gardens of shrines and palaces, in particular, would serve as models. Certainly the garden designers and the townsmen themselves must have realized the practical advantages of such gardens.

A third type of courtyard-garden tradition was evolved within the precincts of Buddhist temples, particularly those of subtemples of the Zen sect—that is, the smaller components of a large Zen establishment. The chief contribution of the Zen priests was that they gave added value to the courtyard garden by making it an expression of Buddhist philosophy. In 1477, in a treatise on landscape-garden design, Hannyabo Tessen, chief priest of the Ryoan-ji, wrote: "Thirty thousand leagues should be compressed into a single foot"—a hyperbole that reflects a basic characteristic of Zen gardens. The Zen priests advocated the use of materials near at hand rather than the expenditure of large sums of money to procure and transport fantastically shaped rocks and rare trees. Indeed, Buddhism itself is symbolized in this frugal advice, and it was of such a philosophy that the rock garden and the dry-landscape (*kare sansui*) garden were born. It is neither possible nor necessary here to introduce the gardens of Zen temples one by one, but it is pertinent to point out that those of subtemples and priests' quarters represent yet another type of the courtyard garden we have been discussing, and it will do no harm to offer a few examples.

The garden in front of the priests' quarters at the Ginkaku-ji (Temple of the Silver Pavilion) is familiar to countless people and therefore need not be described here (Plates 43, 44), but it is unlikely that many are acquainted with the one in front of the meditation hall at another Kyoto temple, the Kennin-ji (Plates 45–47). This garden is a small one: an area of fine white gravel in which flagstones serve as walks to connect the surrounding priests' quarters, abbot's quarters, and main entranceway. It is planted with several evergreen trees and clumps of low-growing shrubs.

As we can observe at the Myoshin-ji and the Daitoku-ji, each subtemple of the Zen temple-monastery complex has its buildings arranged in a set pattern. Despite the rigidity of the layout, however, we receive a distinctly different impression as we go from one subtemple to another. The chief reason for the variety of impressions lies in the differing design of the front gardens. Let us look briefly at four of the Daitoku-ji subtemples as instances of varied front-garden design.

When we enter the gate of the Obai-in, what we see directly ahead of us is the entrance to the priests' quarters, but the Koto-in offers a different experience, for its front garden suggests a winding road that leads into mountain recesses. At the Shinju-an we see the entrance to the abbot's quarters straight ahead, while the entrance to the priests' quarters lies at one side. Again, at the Hoshun-in, as we follow the winding path along a tile-roofed clay wall, we come upon a head-on view of the entrance to the temple itself, with only a partial view of the entrance to the priests' quarters at the right.

Indeed, Zen gardens like these have had a great influence on gardens of the present day, but why did the people of Momoyama and Edo times not reproduce such gardens at their residences? Why did they not choose to inherit this tradition and further its development? Of course, it cannot be said that no urban courtyard gardens at all adopted the techniques of the shrine, palace, and temple courtyard gardens described above, but those that did adopt them are so few in number that they may be disregarded.

Here we arrive at a single answer to all our questions in the present chapter. What seems at first glance to be a rather strange phenomenon—that is, the townspeople's predilection for the tea-garden style above all other courtyard-garden styles—becomes quite clear when we understand the great and leading role played by the tea-ceremony culture in the lives of commoners and aristocrats alike. In a word, it was esteem for this culture that dictated the style of the urban courtyard garden.

13: A DISTILLATION OF CULTURE

Wᴴᴇɴ ᴡᴇ ᴅɪsᴄᴜss the tea ceremony, the one thing we must not forget is that this ritual, carried out in a very limited space, represents a distillation of the culture of the age in which it originated. In that age, to master the tea ceremony was not simply to acquire one of the polite accomplishments but also to attain the highest level of achievement in contemporary culture. It was through the tea ceremony that the cultural level of the townspeople was elevated, and the tea masters were the leaders in all matters of design. Today we seem to give attention only to the etiquette of the ceremony, and we tend to forget that it was more than anything else a condensation of all that was best in the culture of late-Muromachi and Momoyama times. The outstanding gardeners of those days were themselves aficionados of tea, and it was through the tea cult that they learned the essence of good garden design.

  Other artists and craftsmen, no less than garden designers, were absorbed in the cult of tea. Even today, the Senke school of tea, which embraces both the Omote Senke and the Ura Senke, employs no fewer than ten families of artist-craftsmen. We can assume that it was only after the Meiji era that these families were limited to ten, and of course all of them have a tradition of employment by the Senke school that antedates that era by a long time. It will be of interest here to list these families and their products.

FAMILY NAME	PRODUCT	FAMILY HEAD
Raku	Raku pottery	Kichizaemon Raku
Onishi	iron teakettles	Seiemon Onishi
Hirai	paper-based lacquerware	Saiemon Hirai

Nakamura	wood-based lacquerware	Sotetsu Nakamura
Okumura	mountings for hanging scrolls	Kichibei Okumura
Kuroda	bamboo ware	Seigen Kuroda
Tsuchida	cloth bags for tea caddies and other utensils	Yuko Tsuchida
Eiraku	porcelain	Zengoro Eiraku
Nakagawa	metalware	Joeki Nakagawa
Komazawa	cabinetwork	Risai Komazawa

These ten families have worked for a number of generations under the leadership of the Senke headmasters, producing tea-ceremony utensils and other appurtenances to their requirements. Although today they place chief emphasis on this aspect of their production, in the past they and other families like them played the roles of leaders in the entire domain of industrial art. It is most important that we remember this fact. Nor is it any less important for us to keep one other fact in mind: when the headmaster placed his own signature on the boxes in which the products of these craftsmen were kept, he signified that it was the tea masters themselves who exerted leadership in craft design.

To learn the ritual of tea meant, first of all, to acquire a basic decorum and a code of manners for the reception and entertainment of guests. The intricate etiquette and the steps in its sequence were not so much technical trivialities as a method for progressing from outward forms to the essential truth of the art of tea. Through such a code of manners the townsmen learned how to play the roles of guests and hosts with assurance and propriety. And every aspect of tea-ceremony etiquette served as a model for the conduct of social intercourse in everyday life: how to dress, how to open a door, how to walk, how to handle the utensils, how to serve a meal and how to eat it, how to carry on a conversation—everything from basic deportment to the preparation and serving of a formal dinner.

The second salient factor to remember in respect of the tea ceremony is that it played a leading role in the interior decoration of urban houses. In the Muromachi period, during the time when upper-class mansions employed the *kaisho-kazari* style—a style of decoration devised for the separate structures where guests were received and entertained—certain craftsmen from among the lower class took part in the interior decoration of tea pavilions, but there was no extension of influence, in this respect, to the houses of urban commoners. In the noblemen's mansions, ornamental screens were placed here and there, triptychs of scroll paintings in Chinese style were hung, imported flower vases of copper were placed on table covers of gold brocade, and brass incense burners rested on similar covers of embroidered brocade. Still, no matter how greatly the noblemen prided themselves on such gorgeousness, what influenced the commoners was nothing more than a single camellia in a plain bamboo vase hanging from a bent nail in the rustically simple clay wall of the tokonoma.

In brief, one decorated the tearoom by placing a hanging scroll and a flower arrangement in the tokonoma. This signified, first, that people not only had an admiration for the arts of calligraphy and painting but also regarded them as a part of one's basic education and, second, that one must become proficient in the art of flower arrangement. Again, even though it was highly stylized, the refined manner of placing the tea-ceremony utensils was a means of elevating one's sense of beauty.

In yet another extension of its influence, the tea ceremony played a leading role in the art of cooking and the fashioning of confections to accompany the tea. Refreshments, of course, are part of the tea ritual, and the meal served during the intermission is known as the *kaiseki*. Kaiseki-style cooking was originally done in the hosts's own household and not by caterers, as is usually the case today. Eventually, such cookery became a trade, and the tea masters, by issuing advice and instructions to the caterers, raised it to the level of an art, so that it became a model for other styles of Japanese cuisine.

During the Muromachi period, among the social circles of the shoguns and the aristocracy, there were such schools of etiquette for banquet cuisine as the Shijo, the Ikuma, and the Ogasawara, and there were such luxurious menus as those for the so-called seven-five-three banquet, in which the first course consisted of seven dishes; the second, of five dishes and two soups; and the third, of three dishes and one soup. But it was in the simple kaiseki menu of one soup, three dishes, and *yuzuke* (boiled rice with hot water poured over it) that people discovered the true essence of cookery. The careful selection of the ingredients and the freshness and refinement with which the food is prepared and served are special characteristics of the kaiseki cuisine.

Again, the confections served with the tea are an indispensable part of the ritual. The most recherché of these came to be known as *jogashi* (elegant confections) in contrast with ordinary ones, which were called *machigashi* (town confections). It is not known since when, but the number of jogashi shops in Kyoto is limited to 248. Among these, the present Tawaraya is a descendant of the former Sawaya in the Muromachi district of the city. Even today it enjoys the patronage of the temples Shokoku-ji, Kinkaku-ji, Ginkaku-ji, Daisho-ji, and Hokyo-ji. In the past, when patrons from such temples visited the shop, they were entertained in the adjoining Itcho-an, which is still there today. The Itcho-an is a 4.5-mat tearoom. Its front, which is open, faces a courtyard garden of some 4 tsubo, or slightly over 13 square meters. In addition to a stone water basin in the center, the garden contains maple and Japanese cedar trees, ferns, bamboo, and a lantern. The tearoom and the garden were designed under the guidance of the Omote Senke school of tea, and the construction of the garden was carried out by Matsumura Toen, who worked under the patronage of the school. And the man who took the leadership in the designing of the Tawaraya's products was the school's headmaster himself.

The fourth and last factor that we must note in our discussion of tea-ceremony influence is the tea garden. It is not necessary here to involve ourselves with the tearoom or the tea garden as such, for we have already noted their chief characteristics and functions. What interests us at this point is the courtyard garden of the urban commoner's house.

Through the medium of the tea ceremony the populace of the Momoyama and Edo periods was able to absorb the essence of contemporary culture. The tea garden, however, was no more than one aspect of the tea cult. Although the courtyard gardens of shrines, of aristocratic residences in the shinden style, and of Zen temples had an excellence of their own, they exerted no influence on the general culture of the common people. In this fact lies the decisive difference between the tea garden and gardens of other types.

Still, as the remarkable popularization of the tea ceremony followed its course, the common people did not take over the tea garden in its original function and form. It was impossible, after all, for them to construct genuine tea gardens within the limited area of their residential lots. Therefore, in the small spaces available among the closely crowded buildings—either at the front of the narrow lot, in the middle, or at the rear—they adapted the technique of the tea garden, producing copies of the original where in fact no such garden could exist. There they placed stone lanterns, steppingstones, and modest trees and shrubs, but this garden was by no means the approach to the nijiri-guchi of the tearoom. The scenery here was meant to be viewed from the interior and, at the same time that it afforded pleasure, the garden was meant to serve the purpose of lighting and ventilation. In this way both the function and the form of the tea garden underwent a transformation.

During approximately a century and a half, from the late 1500's through the mid-1700's, when the art created by the tea masters attained general popularity and permeated every corner of the urban commoner's house, the tea garden thus bore fruit in the guise of the courtyard garden. Today even the most casual small gardens, including those built as recently as ten years ago, cannot exist in disregard of the five-hundred-year history of the tea garden. Among the urban courtyard gardens existing at present, there are none of great age. The oldest of them date back only to the Meiji era, and the majority of them were constructed in the Taisho era and the current Showa era. Even though we may contend that these gardens were designed by modern hands, we can sense in the background the white hands of long-departed tea masters offering gentle guidance and instruction.

14: THREE COMPONENTS OF THE COURTYARD GARDEN

As we have noted, the urban courtyard gardens of the Momoyama and Edo periods were an outgrowth of the popularization of the tea garden. The people of the times, using the tea garden as a model and borrowing three of its component features, together with a number of technical details, created a new genre based on entirely different principles—that is, the tsuboniwa, or courtyard garden, of the urban commoner's house. The three borrowed elements were the steppingstones, the lantern, and the ritual water basin, none of which were found in gardens that antedated the origin of the tea garden. It will be worth our while here to consider these elements one by one.

Steppingstones (Plates 52, 65, 69) were an invention of the tea garden. According to the *Choandoki*, a collection of tea-ceremony anecdotes published in 1640, Ishiguro Dotei, senior disciple of the tea master Murata Juko, initiated the use of steppingstones when he had them placed in the garden of his residence on the outskirts of Kyoto, where he lived in seclusion. The *Choandoki* relates that the shogun Ashikaga Yoshimasa (1435–90), returning one day from a hawking expedition, stopped for a visit at Dotei's hermitage. Probably because the path through the garden was muddy, Yoshimasa had his attendants spread out a number of different things for him to walk on. Seeing this, Dotei conceived the idea of laying flat stones at intervals along the garden path. And from the *Buke Myomokusho*, a record of medieval warrior families, we learn that the daimyo Uesugi Kenshin (1530–78), in the inner compound of his Kasugayama Castle, had a garden spread with gravel in which stepping stones were laid out.

After the beginning of the Edo period it was unthinkable for a tea garden to be without steppingstones, but in the age of the previously noted Jo-o and the greatest of all tea masters, Sen no Rikyu (1521-91)—that is, late Muromachi and Momoyama—such gardens apparently existed. There were, for example, the garden of Rikyu's son-in-law Mozuya Shoan in Kyoto and that of the Shuun-an subtemple of the Nanshu-ji in Sakai.

In gardens without steppingstones, since footgear was likely to become soiled, the path ended at a kind of duckboard of wood or bamboo where guests could remove their wooden clogs or leather-soled sandals and then step up onto a small veranda from which they entered the tearoom by opening the shoji or a low sliding door. In such cases the guests left their clogs and sandals as they were, since they would have dirtied their hands by trying to clean them, and the host dispatched a servant to do the job instead. The above-mentioned Mozuya's tea garden was planted with a lawn that served in place of steppingstones to prevent the soiling of footgear. In any event, the chief function of steppingstones was to avoid muddiness underfoot rather than to add to the attractiveness of the garden.

Rikyu said that steppingstones were sixty percent functional and forty percent aesthetic, while his follower Furuta Oribe (1544-1615) reversed the percentages. In spite of the difference of opinion here, we can assume that steppingstones were introduced into the tea garden because the stroll along the path from the garden entrance to the nijiri-guchi was of great importance to the tea ritual. The dry-landscape garden of the Daisen-in at the Daitoku-ji and the rock garden of the Ryoan-ji were not made for people to walk in, and therefore the idea of steppingstones probably never entered the minds of the designers. To be sure, in the large garden of the Kinkaku-ji (Temple of the Golden Pavilion), which was once part of the Kitayama residence of the shogun Ashikaga Yoshimitsu (1358-1408), people no doubt once walked from building to building, but the designer had no conscious aim of a prescribed path that would provide visitors with an interesting series of spatial experiences. In other words, the Kinkaku-ji garden was not a tea garden, and Yoshimitsu's chief concern at Kitayama was to construct a re-creation of the nobleman's villa of Heian times.

Certainly steppingstones were the product of a new concept inherent in the tea garden, and they underwent a transformation from the purely functional to the aesthetic. The populace of the Edo period introduced them into the rather spacious gardens of shoin-style residences, assigning them both a functional and an aesthetic role, but in courtyard gardens they were treated as purely decorative objects. Since there are virtually no courtyard gardens in which one can walk, there is no functional need for steppingstones. And since such gardens are meant to be viewed from indoors, their steppingstones are quite clearly nothing more than ornaments. If, for example, a tearoom adjoins the courtyard garden, the guests do not approach it by way of the stepping-stones but usually by way of a corridor. This simulation of the tea garden is one of the aspects of its popularization.

As it was with steppingstones, so it was with the lantern: the tea garden was the first to employ it as an element of garden design (Plates 67, 69, 88, 100). At the subtemple Koto-in of the Daitoku-ji is the grave of the warrior, poet, and tea master Hosokawa Sansai (1563–1645), and its marker is a hexagonal stone lantern some 180 centimeters tall. It is said that this lantern was once a cherished possession of Sen no Rikyu and that when both the military dicta-tor Hideyoshi and the daimyo warrior Sansai requested it as a gift, Rikyu deliberately broke off one of the six sections of its curved top and, using the excuse that it would be rude to offer a damaged lantern to Hideyoshi, pre-sented it to Sansai instead. Whether the story is true or not, we can see in it a clear indication of the tea masters' remarkable interest in lanterns.

The tea masters, of course, introduced lanterns into their gardens to pro-vide illumination when the tea ceremony was held at night. In gardens of earlier times—for example, those of the Heian and Kamakura periods—bonfires of pinewood were used for lighting, as we are are reminded in the chronicle *Eiga Monogatari*. It was difficult, however, to use bonfires in a tea garden, first of all because of the danger of conflagration and, second, because the brightness of fire would have destroyed the atmosphere of a mountain hermitage that the tea masters sought to create. What therefore came to attract the attention of the tea masters was the votive lanterns of temples and shrines.

Such lanterns, of course, had been used at Buddhist temples since Nara times. Later, after the beginning of the Heian period, they also came into use as votive lights at Shinto shrines. There are such old examples as a lantern at the Taima-dera in Nara made of stone from Mount Anamushi and the Citron Tree Lantern dedicated by the court aristocrat Fujiwara Tadamichi to the Kasuga Wakamiya Shrine in 1137. The sixteenth century, when the tea cere-mony at length began to attain popularity, was an age of ruin for temples and shrines, for it was also an age of prolonged civil strife that brought wide-spread destruction, and no doubt many stone lanterns were left abandoned on their premises. It is said that Rikyu was the first to find a new purpose for such lanterns by bringing them into the tea garden. A record of the times in-forms us that once in the dead of night, in a cemetery that lay at the foot of the Higashiyama range in the vicinity of Toribeno, Rikyu was attracted by the lights left burning in the stone lanterns. It was this sight that gave him the idea of using stone lanterns for illumination in his garden. There is small doubt that this story is true, for it was part of Rikyu's aesthetic philosophy to discover new value in things that had been abandoned as worthless. Since Rikyu himself wrote in 1587 concerning the role of the lantern in the tea garden, it is safe to assume that by the closing decades of the sixteenth century it had become fairly common as an element of the garden setting. As we have already seen, Matsuya Hisayoshi took note of a lantern burning in the small tea garden of Okaya Doka when he visited Doka in 1591. Similarly, Hisayoshi mentions early-morning visits to Furuta Oribe in the Fushimi district of Kyoto in 1596 and to Kobori Enshu in the Rokujizo district in 1601 and in both instances speaks of the lighted stone lanterns that stood in their tea gardens. In Kyoto the tea masters and other devotees of the tea cult vied with one another to become the owners of well-weathered, moss-covered lanterns, but in outlying areas new lanterns were also made in appropriate tea-garden style.

Although the primary role of the lantern was to furnish nighttime illumination, it played the simultaneous role of enhancing the aesthetic quality of the garden. In view of its dual function, it was assigned to certain specific places: near the interior gate, near the waiting bench, near the ritual water basin, near the sword rack, or near the nijiri-guchi. This is not to say, however, that lanterns are placed in all these positions in any one garden. Since too many lanterns would give the appearance of streetlights and thereby ruin the atmosphere, they are omitted at some of the locations.

In his *Sado Bemmosho,* a tea-ceremony manual for beginners, Yamada Sohen (1627–1708) recommends that three wicks be used in the morning and at night for the oil lamp inside a garden lantern but that four wicks be used on a moonlit night. If we think in terms of function alone, it would seem reasonable to reduce the brightness of lanterns on a moonlit night, but the very fact that the tea masters called for increasing it is clear proof that lanterns were placed in tea gardens not only for illumination but also for aesthetic pleasure. The seclusion and tranquility of the garden was unmistakably enhanced by the somewhat lonely appearance of lantern light seen vaguely among the trees and shrubs.

It was the stone lantern in its decorative aspect that the urban commoners borrowed from the tea garden to add interest to their own courtyard gardens. It thereby lost its functional purpose and, morning or evening, served as nothing more than an element of design intended to give pleasure to the householders and their guests.

The stone water basin (Plates 5, 55, 68, 76, 80) existed as early as the Higashiyama age—the period in the late fifteenth century when, as we have seen, the shogun Ashikaga Yoshimasa served as arbiter of culture. We must note, however, that the shape of the basin—particularly its height—varied with the social status of the persons for whose use it was designed. Noblemen stood erect when they washed their hands in ritual fashion, and therefore a taller basin was required. People of lower rank bent over and thus used basins of shorter height. The tea masters abolished this distinction by employing in their gardens a low stone basin over which every guest, nobleman and commoner alike, had to bend down to wash his hands and rinse his mouth before the tea ceremony.

According to the previously cited *Choandoki,* the earliest teahouses had a water basin in the earth-floored area under the eaves. Although in later times such basins were invariably made of stone, earlier ones were also made of wood and were sometimes nothing more than wooden buckets. When Matsuya Hisashige visited the tea master Sen no Sotan in Kyoto in the spring of 1608, he observed that steppingstones had been laid down in the garden and that an old foundation stone had been converted into a water basin— another example of the discovery of new values in discarded objects. Again, late in 1609, when Matsuya Hisayoshi visited the garden of the celebrated tea master and designer Oda Uraku (pupil of Sen no Rikyu) in the Temman district of Osaka, he noted that it was planted with a lawn and with Japanese cypress trees, arbor vitae, and *maki* (podocarpus) and that its water basin, like the one in Sotan's garden, had once been a foundation stone.

Naturally, since the water in the shallow stone basin was insufficient for washing hands that were actually dirty, its use was symbolic rather than practical. It goes without saying that what was important here was the ritual cleansing of the heart and the mind in preparation for the tea ceremony. Nevertheless, it cannot be said that the water basin had no practical function at all, for at least two of the tea-ceremony classics point out that one need not wash one's hands there in the morning because they are not greasy at that time.

The stone water basin proved to be more effective as a feature of the urban courtyard garden than steppingtones and the stone lantern. It is difficult to create harmony in such a garden by employing steppingstones and a stone lantern alone as the major elements in the design. But when a stone basin and its accompanying stones —the stone for the hot-water bucket, the lamp stone, and the front stones, to give them their tea-garden names—are added to the design, the courtyard garden is neatly "tightened up," so to speak, and becomes properly composed. And when clear, sparkling water brims at the edge of the basin and the green moss on the surrounding stones becomes wet with the overflow, there is an almost poetic purity in the sight. When one looks at the water in an elegant stone basin—a basin neither too large nor too small—he finds there the same deep serenity that he finds on looking into an ancient mirror.

The small, dry courtyard garden often tends to produce a sense of suffocation in the viewer, but once a stone basin has been placed there and filled with crystal-clear water, this alone is enough to generate a feeling of great relief. If it is possible to keep the water flowing into the basin by way of a bamboo conduit, one can create a sense of refreshment in the heat of summer and, in autumn, a true air of rustic beauty.

During the Edo period the tea garden became stylized and tended to be nothing more than a meaningless convention. Meanwhile, for their courtyard gardens, the townsmen extracted from it the three components that we have been discussing here: the steppingstones, the lantern, and the ritual water basin. From the viewpoint of the tea garden itself, which esteemed traditional forms, it may appear that the courtyard garden adapted the three elements in obliviousness of the spirit and significance of the original model—that it was, in fact, nothing more than a fabricated garden. After all, however, there is in the phenomenon of popularization a certain covetousness, a kind of greed that fears nothing. The populace, using these three components of the tea garden in complete disregard of their original function, constructed courtyard gardens that enriched the environment of its own daily life.

15: THE ESSENCE OF THE COURTYARD GARDEN

No MATTER HOW MUCH the courtyard garden resembled the tea garden in style, it had certain characteristic requirements of its own that found no expression in the tea garden. Since it was customary, as it still is today, for urban commoners' houses in Kyoto to front on the street, the *maeniwa,* or front garden, was an exception, although we can cite such examples as the front gardens of the Raku and the Onishi residences (Plates 90, 93). In the Raku garden large steppingstones of rectangular cut are laid in a ground cover of gravel to form a path between plantings of *yatsude* (*Fatsia japonica*) and hemp palms. Since the garden itself here is actually the passage from the gate to the main entrance of the house, it was possible to employ tea-garden techniques of design. There is a difference, however, between front gardens and the two other urban courtyard garden types: the *nakaniwa,* or inner garden—that is, the garden between the component structures of a house—and the *uraniwa,* or rear garden. Let us look for a moment at the nakaniwa as representative of these two.

In the traditional-style houses of Kyoto, large numbers of which survive today, the front part is normally the *mise,* or shop, run by the family, while the living quarters lie to the rear, often beyond an inner garden. In fact, there may even be a second inner garden that separates the living quarters into two parts. Since the inner garden can be viewed from three directions—that is, from the front part of the house, from the corridor connecting front and rear, and from the rear—it must be designed accordingly. Again, since it can also be viewed from the second floor, it must be designed to appear attractive from that angle as well (Plates 82, 83, 85, 86). Naturally, when one sits in a second-floor room and looks out, he sees the tops of the trees in the garden, and this view, too, must be made to give the impression of a picture. In a word, the courtyard garden requires for its appreciation that it be viewed from a number of different directions.

All this is not to say, however, that courtyard gardens of such ideal design can be found in urban districts, for it is unlikely that there are any so perfect as not to call for improvement. Sometimes they are lifeless imitations, sometimes outright frauds, and sometimes concoctions of sheer vulgarity. It is improbable that the techniques of the courtyard garden will ever serve as a model for other forms of garden design.

Still, the important fact to remember about the courtyard garden is that it has never sought to be an ideal or a perfect creation. It is by no means impossible, of course, to construct a garden of this type in which the individuality of the designer is strongly reflected and no further improvement is needed at all. But gardeners and garden designers never strove for perfection in this aspect of garden design, and if perfection had been their aim, they would never have been able to achieve what they called a "good courtyard garden." What they required, then, was a presentable garden and not a perfect one, and in this we see reflected the good sense and the basic philosophy of the urban garden designer of the Edo period. No matter how outlandish or curious a garden he was called on to construct, he never abandoned his judgment, for it was a faculty that he could in no case relinquish. It was, in fact, the ultimate source of his pride.

If we stop to think about it, we can see that a garden is never constructed for the head of the household alone. Even in the strongly feudalistic society of the Edo period, when patriarchal authority dominated the family, there was a sensible recognition of the fact that no garden was meant solely for the master of the house. Other members of the family may well have their opinions concerning the design of the garden. If the husband, for example, says that he wants a tranquil garden, a garden with a stone basin in which the water reflects the blue sky and brings a sense of purity into the heart, the wife may suggest a brighter garden, a garden spread with fine white gravel and planted with a few bamboos and ferns. Again, guests who visit the family and are treated to a view of the courtyard garden will undoubtedly have a variety of opinions and interpretations. If there is one who finds the stone lantern too large and the steppingstones inharmoniously placed, there will be another to point out that a smaller lantern would make a mere miniature of the garden and give it an even smaller look and that the very lack of harmony in the placement of the steppingstones produces a more compact design.

To repeat, the urban courtyard garden is not meant for the enjoyment of one person alone. It gives pleasure to the entire family, and it is, in a sense, the finest of gifts with which to delight visitors. There is no need for it to represent the pinnacle of design. Nor has it ever sought to serve as a model for other types of gardens. Naturally, in assuming this attitude toward design, the courtyard garden opened itself to the possibility of incorporating vulgarities. It was the refined taste of the tea cult and the influence of the tea masters on garden designers that saved it from this degradation, even though, as we have noted, a few vulgar courtyard gardens can be found. In any event, after the finished garden has been criticized this way and that, there finally comes the time when a consensus is reached: "Leave it as it is. Don't try to do anything more with it. This way is best." And this, of course, is what the old-time designers meant by a "good garden."

One cannot aim at a good garden from the start. Indeed, even though one may begin with such an aim, there are too many elements that refuse to obey orders. Man-made objects like lanterns and water basins can be freely selected and kept under control, but stones and gravel, trees and shrubs, and even grass are quite different things. These are all splendid works of art created by nature and, like the works of art created by man, have a decided individuality. Stones, for example, are products of nature that have gone through long centuries of patient weathering. Moreover, like human beings, they have faces and hands and legs and feet. Regardless of their differences in size and type, they have facial expressions, and every stone has a will of its own. Novice gardeners are unable to read the facial expressions of stones, and gardeners with a certain degree of experience know that stones are thoroughly reluctant to obey orders, but master gardeners know how to coax and humor these willful stones into submission. For this reason, when a master gardener sees a stone that some heartless garden owner has ordered to be placed in an obviously upside-down position, he expresses his pity for it by raising its head and lowering its feet, at the same time perhaps saying something like this: "I'm sorry for you. You must have had a rough time of it." If another stone, at the hands of a merciless master, has been made to face the side rather than the front, the gardener shows sympathy for it by righting its position, and we can imagine that he speaks to it like this: "You really suffered, didn't you? From now on, please face this way."

It is the same with trees and other plants. For all their similarity, no two maples trees are ever quite alike, nor are any two ferns. Each plant has its own individual shape, its own personality, its own manner of growth. When their growth becomes disorderly, they must be trimmed and pruned, but this does not mean that they must be forced against their nature—their own will. The master gardener knows this, and when the owner of a garden comments, for example, that the recently planted bamboo seems to be of unattractive shape, he replies, "Bamboo knows how to grow without our telling it what to do" and leaves it exactly as it is. In two or three years, growing according to its own will, the bamboo takes on the graceful shape that the gardener foresaw for it when he admonished the owner.

For such reasons as these, no matter how much one may wish to predetermine the design of a courtyard garden, it is next to impossible to obtain appropriate stones and trees. One may draw the plan with extreme care, but stones and trees have a way of not listening to what the garden owner says. Again, no matter how many stones and trees there might be, one is likely to discover that not a single one of them conforms to his deepest desires. On the other hand, quite by chance, he may come upon a stone that he thinks would have been a far better choice than one that is presently in his courtyard garden. But if he discards the old stone and replaces it with the new one and then, like a man who has unsuccessfully taken a second wife, discovers that he cannot live with it, it is clear that the new stone had no affinity with the garden after all.

It is this way with everything. Consequently, both the gardener and the garden owner must be patient, and the courtyard garden, as though realizing their patience, will take on a perennial beauty that is always new and fresh. If a man respects himself, then he must also respect the trees and stones that nature has created. It was nature itself, maintaining harmony among the countless elements of its own creation, that served as the supreme model for the courtyard garden. Too strict an adherence to forms is equivalent, in the words of an old Japanese proverb, to straightening the horns and killing the cow. In a word, the formalist loses flexibility of mind and heart, and the garden loses its life. For this reason, a good gardener has always tried to refine and enrich his concepts and imaginative ideas, maintaining a flexible attitude to stand him in good stead whenever the occasion arises.

It will not do to use purposely small trees and stones and a purposely small lantern in a courtyard garden simply because the garden itself is small. To employ such a device is only to make the small garden look all the smaller and to give it a pitiful and desolate air. On the contrary, to take trees for an example, large trees are sometimes needed. The upper part of a fairly tall tree that reaches above the second-floor level can be viewed as a kind of painting framed by the windows of upstairs rooms (Plate 86). A natural choice is the maple, which presents its own pageant of the seasons in its changes from the fresh green of spring to the deeper green of summer and then to the bright colors of autumn and, finally, the leafless boughs of winter. Evergreens, though subtler in their changes of color, are also a good choice, for they assume an interesting variety of moods: on a moonlit night, on a rainy day, on a snowy day, under artificial illumination from inside the house.

It should be noted, of course, that such large trees cannot be brought into the courtyard garden after the house has been completed. For this reason, until around the middle of the Meiji era—that is, about 1890—the prospective builder of a house consulted with both his architect-carpenter and his gardener before construction ever got under way. Today, however, the gardener is in most cases called in only after the house has been built and is then asked to create something suitable. But there is usually nothing much than can be done with the space that is left over for the gardener to work with. Since the garden is enclosed, the ventilation is bad, and there is not enough sunlight. Such conditions, of course, are unfavorable to trees and other plants, but one cannot solve the problem by selecting only the strongest of species, for then the garden would take on an all the more gloomy appearance. It is not the species that counts but the appropriateness of the trees and shrubbery to the garden setting.

A courtyard garden requires frequent sprinkling, not only for the good of the plants that grow there but also to enhance the mood of freshness and natural beauty that the garden seeks to create. In summer it may seem logical to sprinkle the more intensely sunlit parts of the garden with a greater amount of water, but such heavy sprinkling will only produce an unpleasant steaminess. It is the shady areas that should be sprinkled more generously, for the garden takes on its most tranquil appearance when the water drips like dew from the ends of the leaves and lies partly dried up on the steppingstones. Perhaps one could say that the garden in such a mood reflects the essence of the tea ceremony.

When the garden is sprinkled on a summer evening, a cool breeze blows refreshingly through the surrounding rooms. In olden times, sprinkling the front garden and the courtyard garden in preparation for the arrival of guests was considered a gracious symbol of welcome.

We are told that there was once a beautiful nun who lived at a Buddhist nunnery in the Osaka district. It was not only her beauty that commanded admiration, for she was also charming in manner and elegant in deportment, and we may surmise that she treated her guests with the utmost refinement. Let us suppose that one day a man visited the nunnery on some business or other. If the nun who received him at the guest entrance was an ugly one, so much the better for effect. After presenting the letter of introduction he had brought with him, he was asked to wait for a few minutes. But the few minutes stretched from five to ten to fifteen, and then, when he had reached the point of exasperation, he was finally asked to step inside. He was ushered into the tearoom, where water was boiling in the kettle and the fragrance of incense filled the air. It was early autumn, and outdoors the cicadas were singing. Now the sliding partitions opened, and the beautiful nun entered the room. All this was a most carefully thought out and irresistibly tasteful performance.

The courtyard garden strives for a similar dramatic effect. In the bustling arcaded street of Sanjo-dori in Kyoto the shop-residences and inns stand side by side with latticed sliding doors at the front of the narrow passages that run between them. Let us glance for a moment at the inn called the Daimonjiya. Beyond the latticed door stretches a long granite-paved passage whose flagstones have been freshly sprinkled (Plate 75). At right in the background, where the passage ends, we see the main entrance to the inn, half concealed in the shadows. There is an unexpected quiet here in the midst of the large and noisy city. When we proceed beyond the main entrance, we see first a courtyard garden alongside the banquet room, then another and still another along the shadowy corridor that connects the rooms, and finally still another where the corridor ends at the last room of the series (Plates 76–78). The rhythmic alteration of light and darkness offers the guests a small but altogether pleasant surprise as they walk from the main entrance to the rear of the inn.

The courtyard gardens of all urban houses follow more or less this same pattern and technique: a bright garden beyond the rather dark earth-floored passage leading from the shop at the front to the main living quarters, another bright garden beside the narrow and shadowed corridor leading from the main living quarters to the deep-eaved rear wing of the house, and a third garden between the rear wing and the stone storehouse at the back of the lot. Such sequential arrangements of garden spaces are not limited to the urban houses of Kyoto alone, for they are quite common in other Japanese cities as well. It is not enough, however, to enjoy the courtyard garden in isolation from its surroundings. It achieves its true virtue as a source of pleasure only when it is viewed in the context of such structural elements as the shadowy earth-floored area leading from the front of the house, the corridor, the adjacent rooms, the veranda, and the narrow passage lying alongside the house.

Courtyard gardens like these, if left unattended, will become waste places within two or three years. A garden is a living thing, and a good garden can only exist only when its owner gives it constant care. A garden, in fact, is a mirror that reflects the owner's heart and his family's way of life. For this reason, in earlier days, the gardener was a frequent visitor at the urban residence. Usually he came alone to have a look at the garden, but occasionally he brought workmen with him—for example, when it was time to trim the trees and shrubbery. Often he would say, "Just let me have a look." Then he would sit for quite some time, smoking his pipe and concentrating on the garden, but such inaction never meant that he was idling. He was busy listening to what the trees and the stones and the garden itself had to say. Since he was such a frequent visitor, it was natural that he should become friendly with the mistress of the house. Just as the chauffeur came to know the husband's secrets, so the gardener came to know those of the wife and was therefore closer to the family than all the other workers and tradesmen it employed. In fact, the wife often requested him to do other things besides taking care of the garden—for example, to replace the winter fittings of the house with those used in summer and vice versa, to help with the annual housecleaning, to straighten out the articles kept in the storehouse, and even to accompany her on shopping excursions. All these were included among the gardener's tasks. In Tokyo, on ceremonial occasions like weddings and funerals, work like checking the guests' outdoor footgear at the entrance was assigned to groups of young men under the direction of a leader, but in Kyoto such tasks were undertaken by the gardener. Interestingly enough, the best way for the gardener to understand the fundamental spirit of garden making was not to learn the etiquette of the tea ceremony but to sit down and drink tea in the ordinary fashion with the family that employed his services. And here, perhaps, we find symbolized the true essence of the courtyard garden as it took form in the urban residences of Kyoto.

1. Courtyard garden, Yamato Bunkakan art museum, Nara.

2. *Detail of borrowed-landscape garden, Jiko-in,*
   Yamato Koriyama, Nara Prefecture.

3. *Detail of tea garden, Shoka-do, Iwashimizu*
   Hachiman Shrine, Kyoto.

4. *View of Upper Garden and borrowed scenery, Shugaku-in, Kyoto.*

5. Ritual water basin and accompanying stones, Shoka-do tea garden, Iwashimizu Hachiman Shrine, Kyoto.

6. *View of Mount Hiei from Shoden-ji temple garden, Kyoto.*

7. *View of Lake Biwa from Tennenzue-tei, Otsu, Shiga Prefecture.*

8. *View of Arashiyama from garden of Kitcho restaurant, Kyoto.*

9. Rin'un-tei, Shugaku-in, Kyoto.

10. *View from Upper Garden, Shugaku-in, Kyoto.*

11. *View from Rin'un-tei, Shugaku-in, Kyoto.*

12. View across Pond of the Bathing Dragon, Upper Garden, Shugaku-in, Kyoto.

13. View from north shore of pond, Upper Garden, Shugaku-in, Kyoto.

14. *Main gate, Middle Garden, Shugaku-in, Kyoto.*

15. Chinese-style bridge, Upper Garden, Shugaku-in, Kyoto.

16. Path leading to Middle Garden, Shugaku-in, Kyoto.

17. View of Entsu-ji temple garden, Kyoto.

18. View of Mount Hiei from Entsu-ji garden, Kyoto.

19. *Shrubbery at front gate, Entsu-ji, Kyoto.*

20. *Pond and garden paths, Murin-an, Kyoto.*

21. *Murin-an garden, Kyoto.*

22. *Detail of pond and shore, Murin-an garden, Kyoto.*

23. *Murin-an garden, Kyoto.*

24. *Brook and rocks, Shinshin-an garden, Kyoto.*

25. Island and stone pagoda, Shinshin-an garden, Kyoto.

26. Cryptomeria grove, Shinshin-an garden, Kyoto.

27. View of main gate, Nanzen-ji temple, from Shinshin-an garden, Kyoto.

28. Detail of Joju–in garden, Kiyomizu–dera, Kyoto.

29. *Borrowed scenery, Joju-in garden, Kiyomizu-dera, Kyoto.*

30. Tenryu-ji temple, Kyoto.

31. Rock arrangement and detail of pond, Tenryu-ji garden, Kyoto.

32. *Borrowed scenery, Tenryu-ji garden, Kyoto.*

33. *Borrowed scenery, Tenryu-ji garden, Kyoto.*

34. *Approach to Jiko-in garden, Yamato Koriyama, Nara Prefecture.*

35. *Borrowed scenery, Jiko-in garden, Yamato Koriyama, Nara Prefecture.*

36. Borrowed scenery, Jiko-in garden, Yamato Koriyama, Nara Prefecture.

37. *View of Great South Gate, Todai-ji temple, from Isui-en garden, Nara.*

38. Isui-en garden and borrowed scenery, Nara.

39. Pond and steppingstones, Isui-en garden, Nara.

40. Detail of courtyard garden, Kyoto Imperial Palace.

41. *Courtyard garden, Ninna-ji temple, Kyoto.*

42. *Courtyard garden, Kamigamo Shrine, Kyoto.*

43. Courtyard garden, priests' quarters, Ginkaku-ji, Kyoto.

44. *Detail of garden, Ginkaku-ji, Kyoto.*

45. *Courtyard garden, meditation hall, Kennin-ji, Kyoto.*

46. Courtyard garden, meditation hall, Kennin-ji, Kyoto.

47. *Detail of courtyard garden, meditation hall, Kennin-ji, Kyoto.*

48. *Courtyard garden, Hossho-in, Ishiyama-dera, Otsu, Shiga Prefecture.*

49. *Courtyard garden, Hossho-in, Ishiyama-dera, Otsu, Shiga Prefecture.*

50. *Steppingstone paths in courtyard garden, Ryosoku-in, Kennin-ji, Kyoto.*

51. *Stone-paved path in tea garden, Ura Senke, Kyoto.*

52. Tea-garden path, Ura Senke, Kyoto.

53. *Tea-garden path leading to waiting booth, Ura Senke, Kyoto.*

54. *Approach to teahouse, Ura Senke, Kyoto.*

55. *Ritual water basin and accompanying stones, Ura Senke, Kyoto.*

56. *Detail of rear garden, Ura Senke, Kyoto.*

57. *Detail of tea garden, Ura Senke, Kyoto.*

58. Detail of garden and surrounding veranda, Ura Senke, Kyoto.

59. *Detail of courtyard garden, Ura Senke, Kyoto.*

60. *Approach to main entrance, Omote Senke, Kyoto.*

61. *Detail of main entrance, Omote Senke, Kyoto.*

62. Window-gate in tea garden, Omote Senke, Kyoto.

63. Steppingstone arrangement in tea garden, Omote Senke, Kyoto.

64. Detail of tea garden, Omote Senke, Kyoto.

65. Steppingstone path in tea garden, Omote Senke, Kyoto.

66. *Stone-paved walk and waiting bench, Kankyu-an, Mushanokoji Senke, Kyoto.*

67. *Detail of tea garden, Kankyu-an, Mushanokoji Senke, Kyoto.*

68. *Ritual water basin and accompanying stones, Yabunouchi school of tea, Kyoto.*

69. *Tea-garden path, Yabunouchi school of tea, Kyoto.*

70. *Detail of tea-garden path, Yabunouchi school of tea, Kyoto.*

71. *Under-eaves area and waiting bench, Hyo-tei restaurant, Kyoto.*

72. *Approach to teahouse, Hyo-tei restaurant, Kyoto.*

73. *Tea-garden pond, Hyo-tei restaurant, Kyoto.*

74. *Exterior of teahouse, Hyo-tei restaurant, Kyoto.*

75. *Approach to main entrance, Daimonjiya inn, Kyoto.*

76. Courtyard garden adjacent to main entrance, Daimonjiya inn, Kyoto.

77. *Guest-room courtyard garden in tea-garden style, Daimonjiya inn, Kyoto.*

78. Guest-room courtyard garden in Zen style, Daimonjiya inn, Kyoto.

79. *Sarusawa Pond, Nara.*

80. Detail of courtyard garden, Yanagi-jaya restaurant, Nara.

81. *Courtyard garden, Yanagi-jaya restaurant, Nara.*

82. *Courtyard garden, Suppon Dai-ichi restaurant, Kyoto.*

83. *Courtyard garden, Suppon Dai-ichi restaurant, Kyoto.*

84. Detail of courtyard garden, Suppon Dai-ichi restaurant, Kyoto.

85. *Detail of courtyard garden, Takeka inn, Kyoto.*

86. Second-floor view of courtyard garden, Takeka inn, Kyoto.

87. Courtyard garden, Sumiya, Kyoto.

88. *Courtyard garden, Warajiya restaurant, Kyoto.*

89. *Courtyard garden, Shibata residence, Kyoto.*

90. *Front courtyard garden, Raku shop-residence, Kyoto.*

91. *Detail of courtyard garden, Zenta shop–residence, Kyoto.*

92. Detail of courtyard garden in front of storehouse, Zenta shop-residence, Kyoto.

93. *Courtyard garden, Onishi residence, Kyoto.*

94. Detail of courtyard garden, Tabata residence, Kyoto.

95. *Stone wall and graveled garden path, Yoda residence, Kyoto.*

96. Rear garden, Yoda residence, Kyoto.

97. Detail of courtyard garden, Uno residence, Kyoto.

98. *Steppingstones and garden shrubs, Uno residence, Kyoto.*

99. *Front garden of Kato shop-residence, Kyoto.*

100. Courtyard garden, Kiyomizu shop–residence, Kyoto.

101. *Outer walls of Shinto priests' residences, Kamigamo Shrine, Kyoto.*

102. Front courtyard garden of Shinto priest's residence, Kamigamo Shrine, Kyoto.

103. Detail of tea garden, Ura Senke, Kyoto.

COMMENTARIES ON THE PHOTOGRAPHS

1. Courtyard garden, Yamato Bunkakan art museum, Nara. This garden, enclosed by glass walls and planted solely with giant bamboos in a spread of white gravel, forms the center of the building. It is viewed here from the main-floor level.

2. Detail of borrowed-landscape garden, Jiko-in, Yamato Koriyama, Nara Prefecture. For its borrowed scenery the Jiko-in garden incorporates an expansive view of the Yamato Plain and the distant mountains that surround it. Beyond the stretch of white gravel in the foreground, a luxuriant clump of closely trimmed azaleas forms a mound of green and deep pink. (See also Plates 34–36.)

3. Detail of tea garden, Shoka-do, Iwashimizu Hachiman Shrine, Kyoto. The Shoka-do was once the residence of the Edo-period painter and man of letters Shokado Shojo. Its tranquil tea garden reflects the rustic but elegant simplicity that characterized the taste of the early tea masters. (See also Plate 5.)

4. View of Upper Garden and borrowed scenery, Shugaku-in, Kyoto. The most celebrated of Japan's borrowed-landscape gardens is the Upper Garden of the Shugaku-in imperial villa. Here the borrowed scenery of hills and mountains is viewed across the Pond of the Bathing Dragon. (See also Plates 9–16.)

5. Ritual water basin and accompanying stones, Shoka-do tea garden. In typical tea-garden style, this ritual water basin stands among a group of stones traditionally known as the lamp stone, the stone for the hot-water bucket, and the front stones. The steppingstone approach to the basin leads in from the foreground. Another detail of the Shoka-do garden appears in Plate 3.

6. View of Mount Hiei from Shoden-ji temple garden, Kyoto. The tile-topped wall of whitewashed clay serves as a trimming line for the borrowed scenery of distant Mount Hiei.

7. View of Lake Biwa from Tennenzue-tei, Otsu, Shiga Prefecture. Here the famous lake that lies northeast of Kyoto is captured as the borrowed scenery of the garden surrounding the Tennenzue-tei, or Pavilion of Natural Pictures. The borrowed scenery also includes a view of Mount Mikami.

8. View of Arashiyama from garden of Kitcho restaurant, Kyoto. The Kitcho garden, like that of the nearby Tenryu-ji temple, borrows the scenery of Arashiyama as part of its design.

9. Rin'un-tei, Shuagku-in, Kyoto. The Rin'un-tei, whose name means "cloud-neighboring pavilion," stands at the highest point in the Upper Garden and commands the finest view of the vast landscape that forms the borrowed scenery of the garden (Plates 4, 10–13).

10. View from Upper Garden, Shugaku-in. Here a maple tree frames the grand panorama of hills and mountains lying to the west. In the right foreground, part of the pond is seen.

11. View from Rin'un-tei, Shugaku-in. On a clear day the borrowed scenery to the west seems to be of almost infinite reach as the distant mountains rise tier on tier beyond the hills in the middle ground.

12. View across Pond of the Bathing Dragon, Upper Garden, Shugaku-in. In this view the mountains to the north are faintly seen in the remote background. A path runs along the top of the dike that retains the pond (top of photograph). In summer, water lilies strike a decorative note among the predominantly green tones of the garden.

13. View from north shore of pond, Upper Garden, Shugaku-in. Here the hills to the east of the garden play the role of borrowed scenery, and the instrument of capture is the sky itself. The structure in the right foreground is a boathouse with a bamboo-and-bark-shingle roof.

14. Main gate, Middle Garden, Shugaku-in. Inside the gate a spread of fine white gravel adds a certain luster to the surrounding greenery. This enclosed garden once contained the relocated palace of the imperial consort Tofukumon-in, wife of the emperor Gomizuno-o.

15.   Chinese-style bridge, Upper Garden, Shugaku-in. A backdrop of luxuriantly forested mountains rises just beyond the place where this Chinese-style bridge connects two islands in the pond. The rather grandiose bridge, constructed more than a century and a half after the garden was completed, violates the emperor Gomizuno-o's original design for a garden in which man-made structures were not to obtrude.

16.   Path leading to Middle Garden, Shugaku-in. In the background, above the pine trees that border the graveled path, the mountains to the north are captured as borrowed scenery. The approach to the Middle Garden, as shown here, is from the background to the foregrand.

17.   View of Entsu-ji temple garden, Kyoto. The Entsu-ji, located in the hilltop village of Hataeda in the suburbs of Kyoto, is a memento of a villa built there in the mid-seventeenth century for the emperor Gomizuno-o. The garden, whose borrowed scenery embraces a view of Mount Hiei (Plate 18), is a small moss garden with some forty stones and various clumps of shrubbery, all carefully laid out but completely natural in appearance.

18.   View of Mount Hiei from Entsu-ji garden. Here the trunks of cryptomerias and Japanese cypress trees, together with that of one red pine, serve as a device to capture a striking view of Mount Hiei as the borrowed scenery of the garden. The hedge in the foreground constitutes the trimming line.

19.   Shrubbery at front gate, Entsu-ji. The carefully trimmed shrubbery stands in a spread of fine gravel with islands of moss. The warm-toned clay wall, topped with tile, blends excellently with the natural stones and the greenery of the garden.

20.   Pond and garden paths, Murin-an, Kyoto. The garden of the Murin-an villa is a stroll garden, designed to provide a succession of attractive views as one walks along its paths. The pond is bordered by carefully selected rocks and clumps of low-growing shrubbery.

21.   Murin-an garden. To capture the scenery of the Higashiyama range of hills for this spacious garden, the designer Jihei Ogawa used two small forests that stand in the background of the garden. The layout is so arranged that the borrowed scenery is viewed through a notch between the two stands of trees.

22.   Detail of pond and shore, Murin-an garden. The shallow pond is fed by a small brook that enters the garden at a higher level in the sloping terrain. The Murin-an villa and its garden were constructed for the famous Meiji-era military and political leader Aritomo Yamagata.

23.   Murin-an garden. As one strolls along the garden paths, the borrowed scenery of the Higashiyama range is viewed from a number of different angles. Here the crest of the range forms an almost horizontal line between the two small forests that draw the distant landscape into the garden.

24.   Brook and rocks, Shinshin-an garden, Kyoto. The pond in the Shinshin-an garden, like that of the Murin-an, is fed by a brook whose quiet murmur enhances the mood of tranquility that the expansive garden evokes.

25.   Island and stone pagoda, Shinshin-an garden. The pond has a central island on which a stone pagoda stands among ferns and low-growing shrubbery. Such pagodas usually have religious connotations, but here the function is purely ornamental. At left an ancient pine tree leans out over the pond.

26.   Cryptomeria grove, Shinshin-an garden. The north side of the garden is occupied by a grove of cryptomeria trees, and the ground beneath them, apparently once planted with shrubbery, is now partly spread with fine white gravel. On clear days the trunks of the trees seem to float upward in the sunlight, creating a bright and clean effect. The Shinshin-an villa, built during the Meiji era, is now owned by the electrical-industry magnate Konosuke Matsushita. Its garden, like that of the Murin-an, was designed by Jihei Ogawa.

27.   View of main gate, Nanzen-ji temple, from Shinshin-an garden. The borrowed scenery of the garden embraces the huge triple gate of the Nanzen-ji, the hills Yokaku and Dokushu, and the Ayato Forest. The capturing device is a woods made up principally of pine trees.

28.   Detail of Joju-in garden, Kiyomizu-dera, Kyoto. There is an air of both elegance and geniality in this small garden of the priests' quarters at Kiyomizu-dera. Aside from the borrowed scenery (Plate 29), the rockwork is of particular interest here.

29.   Borrowed scenery, Joju-in garden. On the side of a small nameless hill a stone lantern has been placed in the midst of the borrowed scenery itself as a device for drawing it into the garden. The hedge in the middle ground serves as the trimming line. In an instant, so to speak, the small space of the garden is expanded through the magic of the stone lantern that captures the hill.

30.   Tenryu-ji temple, Kyoto. The Tenryu-ji was established at Arashiyama in 1345 as a memorial temple for the ill-fated Emperor Godaigo, who set up a rival court in the mountains of Yoshino in 1337 and died there in 1339.

31. Rock arrangement and detail of pond, Tenryu-ji garden. Here the pond reflects the abbot's quarters, in front of which the garden lies. The Tenryu-ji and its garden were once the site of a tenth-century imperial villa and, later, of the thirteenth-century Kameyama Palace, where the retired emperor Gosaga resided.

32. Borrowed scenery, Tenryu-ji garden. On the far side of the pond, behind the low hill called Kameyama, the cherry trees and maples of Arashiyama enter the garden design in the role of borrowed scenery. In the foreground is the section of the garden that lies immediately in front of the abbot's quarters.

33. Borrowed scenery, Tenryu-ji garden. The rock arrangements in the foreground, suggestive of an ink painting in the Chinese style of the Northern Sung dynasty, serve to draw the borrowed landscape of Arashiyama into the garden design.

34. Approach to Jiko-in garden, Yamato Koriyama, Nara Prefecture. A stone-paved path with a bamboo railing leads through a setting that suggests remote mountains and solitary valleys.

35. Borrowed scenery, Jiko-in garden. At the Jiko-in the posts and eaves of the broad veranda join with the trimming line of the hedge to frame an imposing view of the Yamato Plain.

36. Borrowed scenery, Jiko-in garden. In offering another view of the borrowed landscape of the Yamato Plain, the Jiko-in garden uses the trunks of pine trees as a capturing device.

37. View of Great South Gate, Todai-ji temple, from Isui-en garden, Nara. For its borrowed scenery, the Isui-en garden captures the Great South Gate of the Todai-ji and the so-called Three Hills of Nara. The device that effects the capture is the woods of the Himuro Shrine. In the background the crest of the hill Wakakusayama rises behind the roof of the gate.

38. Isui-en garden and borrowed scenery. In this panoramic view the pond lies in the foreground, while the middle ground is occupied by gently molded and luxuriantly planted terrain. In the background, beyond the woods of the Himuro Shrine, the roof of the Great South Gate soars into the skyline of grassy hills.

39. Pond and steppingstones, Isui-en garden. The steppingstones are mementos of the garden's original seventeenth-century owner, for they once served as mortars in preparing the sizing for the fine-quality ramie cloth in which he traded.

40. Detail of courtyard garden, Kyoto Imperial Palace. In the days of the ancient court, the residences of emperors and noblemen were graced with simple courtyard gardens like this one: a spread of fine white gravel planted here and there with clumps of *hagi,* or bush clover. Other plants used in such gardens included *sasa* (bamboo grass) and *yomogi* (artemisia).

41. Courtyard garden, Ninna-ji temple, Kyoto. This small enclosed garden is planted with bamboo grass in a carpet of moss and ornamented with a few carefully selected stones. At left is a wooden lantern of antique style.

42. Courtyard garden, Kamigamo Shrine, Kyoto. In Shinto gardens like this one the whiteness of the ground cover of fine gravel symbolizes purity. The two cones of molded sand may be considered to represent islands in a calm sea.

43. Courtyard garden, priests' quarters, Ginkaku-ji, Kyoto. At the end of the long, narrow approach to the Ginkaku-ji (Temple of the Silver Pavilion), visitors come upon this tranquil garden in front of the priests' quarters. The temple, authentically known as the Jisho-ji, is the site of the famous Silver Pavilion, built for the shogun Ashikaga Yoshimasa (1435–90), sponsor of the Higashiyama culture.

44. Detail of garden, Ginkaku-ji. Natural stones, fine white gravel, moss, azaleas, and evergreens compose a quiet corner of the garden. The gravel is raked to form a wavelike pattern that suggests ripples in a stream.

45. Courtyard garden, meditation hall, Kennin-ji, Kyoto. In this small Zen-temple garden, flagstone walks lead through the ground cover of fine white gravel to connect the meditation hall with the other surrounding buildings. The few plants in the garden include several evergreen trees and clumps of low-growing shrubbery. The dominant mood here is one of brightness and clarity.

46. Courtyard garden, meditation hall, Kennin-ji. Here the flagstone walks separate the white-gravel area of the garden from the area carpeted with dark-green moss. There is a certain sculptural quality in the trees and shrubbery of this bright and placid garden.

47. Detail of courtyard garden, meditation hall, Kennin-ji. The contemplative mood inspired by the garden is symbolized here by a small planting of *aogiri* (*Firmiana platanifolia*) in the expanse of fine gravel.

48. Courtyard garden, Hossho-in, Ishiyama-dera, Otsu, Shiga Prefecture. Trees

on a mossy island in a stretch of white gravel form a screen for the building in the background. The flat square-cut steppingstones make an inviting path to the entrance. Legend says that the eleventh-century court lady Murasaki Shikibu wrote part of her celebrated novel *The Tale of Genji* at the Ishiyama-dera.

49. Courtyard garden, Hossho-in, Ishiyama-dera. The glowing white of the fine gravel, the steppingstones, and the clay walls contrasts vividly with the dark green of the pine trees and the moss.

50. Steppingstone paths in courtyard garden, Ryosoku-in, Kennin-ji, Kyoto. The gardens of Zen temples customarily use steppingstones of geometrical shape. The Ryosoku-in is a subtemple of the Kennin-ji, the garden of whose meditation hall is pictured in Plates 45–47.

51. Stone-paved path in tea garden, Ura Senke, Kyoto. In contrast with the Zen garden, the tea garden shows a preference for stones of natural shape, whether they are used as steppingstones or as stones in a paved walk like the one seen here. Ura Senke is both a school of the tea ceremony and the residence of the current master of the school.

52. Tea-garden path, Ura Senke. Steppingstones and stone-paved paths are both inventions of the tea garden. The two are often combined, as in the example shown here. The ground cover is a carpet of moss.

53. Tea-garden path leading to waiting booth, Ura Senke. Here the path, consisting partly of closely placed stones and partly of steppingstones, leads to the waiting booth, where tea-ceremony guests gather to await the host's invitation to enter the teahouse.

54. Approach to teahouse, Ura Senke. Steppingstones lead to the low sliding-door aperture (extreme left) through which guests enter the teahouse. The brushwood-and-bamboo fence enhances the purposely rustic atmosphere.

55. Ritual water basin and accompanying stones, Ura Senke. This stone water basin, carved on its four sides with images of the Buddhas of the Four Directions, was no doubt retrieved from an abandoned temple site. It harmonizes perfectly with the natural stones that surround it in this quiet corner of the tea garden.

56. Detail of rear garden, Ura Senke. In this small garden, a graveled path is bordered by a miniature grove of bamboo. At extreme right, an antique bronze lantern stands on a pedestal of carved stone.

57. Detail of tea garden, Ura Senke. This garden might easily be mistaken for the garden of an ordinary urban residence, although a closer look reveals the deliberately rustic atmosphere of the tea garden. The bamboo-and-wood bench at lower right has a particularly rural air.

58. Detail of garden and surrounding veranda, Ura Senke. There is a clear indication here of the rustic elegance that Muromachi-period townsmen sought to express in their gardens. It goes almost without saying that the hand of the tea master is everywhere apparent in the design.

59. Detail of courtyard garden, Ura Senke. Among evergreen plants, the shrub *nanten* (*Nandina domestica*) is especially suitable for the courtyard garden. Its clusters of red berries, produced late in autumn, add to its attractiveness.

60. Approach to main entrance, Omote Senke, Kyoto. The stone-paved walk is bordered by beds of gravel and screens of shrubbery clipped to resemble walls. Omote Senke is both a school of the tea ceremony and the residence of the current master of the school.

61. Detail of main entrance, Omote Senke. Guests approach this small courtyard from the foreground. At right is one of the entrances to the garden. Only a few shrubs are planted here in the bed of gravel.

62. Window-gate in tea garden, Omote Senke. This interesting structure stands across the steppingstone path that leads through the outer to the inner tea garden. It is actually a detached clay wall with a windowlike aperture through which guests pass as they approach the teahouse in the inner garden, and it symbolizes the division between the everyday world outside and the tranquil world of the tea ceremony.

63. Steppingstone arrangement in tea garden, Omote Senke. At the gate where the tea master greets his guests, two large steppingstones are placed in a bed of smaller stones, one on either side of the sill. All the stones in this arrangement are of natural shape.

64. Detail of tea garden, Omote Senke. There is a clear suggestion here of what the Japanese like to call *shinzan yukoku:* distant mountains and solitary valleys.

65. Steppingstone path in tea garden, Omote Senke. The casual-looking but carefully studied placement of the stones in their bed of moss gives the feeling of a path through a natural woodland glade. After their introduction into the tea

garden in the late fifteenth century, steppingstones became an almost indispensable element in other types of Japanese gardens.

66. Stone-paved walk and waiting bench, Kankyu-an, Mushanokoji Senke, Kyoto. A walk paved with natural and cut stone leads past the waiting bench at left. The Kankyu-an is a teahouse on the premises of Mushanokoji Senke, which is both a school of the tea ceremony and the residence of the current master of the school.

67. Detail of tea garden, Kankyu-an, Mushanokoji Senke. The refreshing green of massed foliage suggests a quiet corner of an undisturbed forest. The stone lantern at upper left is almost wholly concealed by the surrounding shrubbery.

68. Ritual water basin and accompanying stones, Yabunouchi school of tea, Kyoto. A round moss-covered basin of natural stone, furnished with a cover and a dipper of unpainted wood, stands in a tranquil woodland setting of ferns and aspidistras.

69. Tea-garden path, Yabunouchi school of tea. Here the path is scattered with fallen gardenia leaves and blossoms. The steppingstones, although they have been placed with studied care, have the look of natural outcrops. In the background a stone tied with rope indicates that the path beyond this point is not to be followed. A square stone lantern, partly covered with lichens, indicates a turning point in the path that enters the scene from the foreground.

70. Detail of tea-garden path, Yabunouchi school of tea. In another part of the garden the path is bordered by aspidistra plants whose glossy leaves reflect the sunlight that spills down through the trees.

71. Under-eaves area and waiting bench, Hyo-tei, Kyoto, The Hyo-tei is an elegant restaurant in the Nanzenji Kusakawa-cho district of Kyoto. This view of one of its buildings shows the broad eaves that are characteristic of the *sukiya*, or teahouse, style of Japanese architecture. The area under the eaves is considered to belong as much to the interior as to the exterior of the building.

72. Approach to teahouse, Hyo-tei. A stone-paved walk leads past a ritual water basin placed among the exposed roots of the neighboring trees. In the background a wood-and-paper lantern uses a sawed-off tree trunk for its pedestal. The scene represents the height of the elegant rusticity for which the early tea masters strove.

73. Tea-garden pond, Hyo-tei. The water in the pond suggests both the quiet

depths of a forest pool and the crystal clarity of a spring. Here the pond is inhabited by a school of carp.

74. Exterior of teahouse, Hyo-tei. The benchlike structure of wood and bamboo is a small veranda upon which the *shoji* (extreme left) open to give a view of the garden. Slightly left of center is the *nijiri-guchi,* the low sliding-door aperture through which guests enter the teahouse. The building seen here is one of four teahouses on the premises of the Hyo-tei. Like the others, it is used for the serving of the tea-ceremony cuisine, or *kaiseki,* in which the restaurant specializes.

75. Approach to main entrance, Daimonjiya inn, Kyoto. Arriving guests reach the main entrance by way of a stone-paved passage that leads in from the street. The inn is located on bustling Sanjo-dori, an avenue in downtown Kyoto.

76. Courtyard garden adjacent to main entrance, Daimonjiya. This is one of four courtyard gardens that add great charm to the traditional-style Daimonjiya inn. Like almost all the urban courtyard gardens of Kyoto, it takes its inspiration from the tea garden. Water flows into the stone basin through a bamboo pipe, adding a pleasant sound effect to the visual attractions of the garden.

77. Guest-room courtyard garden in tea-garden style, Daimonjiya. Here an antique stone guidepost has been retrieved as an ornament for a tiny courtyard garden that lies outside one of the guest rooms of the inn.

78. Guest-room courtyard garden in Zen style, Daimonjiya. Beyond the veranda, bamboos, ferns, and other plants grow in a spread of fine white gravel. On its outer side, the garden is enclosed by a tall fence of bark strips and bamboo rods.

79. Sarusawa Pond, Nara. The Yanagi-jaya restaurant, details of whose gardens are shown in Plates 80 and 81, stands on the shore of this large tree-bordered pond in Nara Park.

80. Detail of courtyard garden, Yanagi-jaya. In this garden the water basin is a natural stone in which a small circular depression has been carved. Among the surrounding stones are two (extreme left) that once served as mortars. An ornamental roof tile (left of center) also adds interest to the setting. The tea-garden influence is particularly evident here.

81. Courtyard garden, Yanagi-jaya. Like other courtyard gardens, this one is designed to be viewed from several different locations in the buildings that enclose it. The stone object in the foreground, carved in the shape of a stylized lotus blos-

som, may once have been the base for a Buddhist image. The bamboo-lattice window seen in the background is a characteristic feature of teahouse architecture.

82. Courtyard garden, Suppon Dai-ichi restaurant, Kyoto. The Suppon Dai-ichi is noted for traditional cookery that features *suppon,* or fresh-water turtle, in a variety of dishes. One of its courtyard gardens is dominated by a large evergreen oak that rises above the complex of surrounding structures and seems to express the dignity of this old established restaurant.

83. Courtyard garden, Suppon Dai-ichi. Another of the restaurant's gardens is planted mainly with *maki* (podocarpus) and *aoki* (*Aucuba japonica*). In addition to its aesthetic function the courtyard garden has the function of providing ventilation and light.

84. Detail of courtyard garden, Suppon Dai-ichi. Here the garden seen from above in Plate 83 is viewed from one of the verandas, and the tea-garden influence is readily apparent. A large pottery vat takes the place of the ritual water basin. The normal-size stone lantern at left illustrates the point that the courtyard garden does not require ornaments or plants of diminutive size.

85. Detail of courtyard garden, Takeka inn, Kyoto. The only trees in the courtyard garden of this traditional-style inn are maples. Here, as in Plate 86, they are seen lifting their tops to the second-floor level of the enclosing structure.

86. Second-floor view of courtyard garden, Takeka. When the *shoji* of this second-floor room are opened, the tops of the maple trees in the courtyard garden are seen beyond the narrow veranda. A second-floor view of the garden should be no less attractive than a first-floor view.

87. Courtyard garden, Sumiya, Kyoto. This is the front courtyard garden of a former *ageya* (brothel)—now a museum piece—in the Shimabara pleasure district of Kyoto. The scene here could very well be the setting for an Edo-period Kabuki play. Although there is only the faintest suggestion of an actual garden, the label of "garden" still applies. At left is a wooden lantern of feudal-period design. The doorway at center is hung with a *noren* (divided curtain) that carries the crest of the establishment.

88. Courtyard garden, Warajiya restaurant, Kyoto. The courtyard garden of this traditional-style restaurant is viewed here through a rope-curtained opening of one of the rooms. In addition to the customary stone lantern and water basin, the garden ornaments include a giant stone toad.

89. Courtyard garden, Shibata residence, Kyoto. This garden displays an interesting combination of the Zen and the tea-garden styles. Islands of moss are placed here and there in the spread of fine white gravel, while potted plants stand on several of the natural stones. At lower right are three tiles of the kind used to ornament the ridge ends of tiled roofs. The pottery basin at extreme right contains goldfish, and its wire-mesh cover is a protection against marauding cats. It is interesting to note that the owner of the residence is a maker of bows for Japanese-style archery.

90. Front courtyard garden, Raku shop-residence, Kyoto. Rectangular slabs of cut stone laid in a bed of gravel form the approach to the main entrance, where a divided curtain carries the announcement that this is the shop-residence of the famous Raku family of potters. The most prominent garden plants are *yatsude* (*Fatsia japonica*), at right, and hemp palms, at left. Although tea-garden techniques have been employed here, there is no resemblance to the tea garden per se.

91. Detail of courtyard garden, Zenta shop-residence, Kyoto. This garden is part of the shop-residence of the old established art dealer Kiichiro Zenta. The large cylindrical stone once served as a base for one of the two pillars of a *torii*—that is, the ceremonial gate to a Shinto shrine.

92. Detail of courtyard garden in front of storehouse, Zenta shop-residence. An antique bronze lantern overshadowed by low-growing bamboo stands on a base of natural stone. In the background is the open door of the storehouse.

93. Courtyard garden, Onishi residence, Kyoto. In many ways this remarkably attractive garden represents the epitome of what an urban courtyard garden should be. The Onishi family, makers of iron teakettles, are among the artist-craftsmen employed by the Senke school of the tea ceremony.

94. Detail of courtyard garden, Tabata residence, Kyoto. Here a *bonsai* (dwarf tree) in a pottery basin occupies a gravel-strewn corner of the garden. Kihachiro Tabata, owner of the residence, is the head of a family of dyers in the famous textile industry of Kyoto.

95. Stone wall and graveled garden path, Yoda residence, Kyoto. A wall of massive stones, laid without mortar in the manner of the foundation walls of Japanese feudal castles, creates an illusion of greater space than the garden actually covers. The wall is topped by a bamboo fence.

96. Rear garden, Yoda residence. In this dry-landscape garden, white stones

scattered among dark-toned rocks simulate a torrent pouring through a mountain glen, while the spread of gravel in the foreground suggests a flowing stream.

97. Detail of courtyard garden, Uno residence, Kyoto. It is characteristic of tea gardens, and of the teahouse-style of architecture as well, that the approach to the entrance of a building should always be a diagonal or a curved line, so that a head-on view is avoided. Here the entranceway is to the right of the path that continues beyond it. The owner of the residence is a well-known ceramic artist.

98. Steppingstones and garden shrubs, Uno residence. The shrubs are planted in a purposely casual fashion to give the illusion of a path across a field. Among the steppingstones is one that once served as a mortar.

99. Front garden of Kato shop-residence, Kyoto. Although it may seem strange to identify this as a garden, considering the fact that it is crowded with garden ornaments, it is actually the front courtyard of the shop-residence of the garden designer Saburo Kato, who works under the professional name of Uekuma. Almost all the objects seen here will be used sooner or later in gardens constructed according to Uekuma's designs.

100. Courtyard garden, Kiyomizu-shop residence, Kyoto. The approach to the living quarters of this long, narrow shop-residence is an inviting courtyard garden. Stone lanterns of two distinctly different types are seen here: at center, a square one resting on a large natural stone; in the background, half hidden by the shrubbery, a more ornate one with a pedestal.

101. Outer walls of Shinto priests' residences, Kamigamo Shrine, Kyoto. Immediately outside the stone-based and tile-topped walls, a flowing stream gives an air of freshness to the tranquil surroundings. The houses built within these walls are occupied by hereditary priests and their families.

102. Front courtyard garden of Shinto priest's residence, Kamigamo Shrine. Perhaps because Shinto priests are also often aficionados of the tea ceremony, the front gardens of their residences at Kamigamo reflect the influence of the tea garden.

103. Detail of tea garden, Ura Senke, Kyoto. The stone lantern and the stone water basin, two indispensable elements of the tea garden, are also symbols of the Kyoto courtyard garden in general, whether at a private residence, an inn, a restaurant, or some other establishment. Here we see these two symbols in the tea garden itself, attractively placed in a setting of shrubbery and trees.

APPENDIX
Locations of Representative Gardens

NOTE: *Asterisks denote gardens illustrated in this book.*

   Byodo-in: Uji Renge, Uji, Kyoto Prefecture
* Daimonjiya inn: Sanjo Kawara-machi Nishi Iru, Nakakyo-ku, Kyoto
   Daisen-in: Daitoku-ji, Daitokuji-cho, Murasakino, Kita-ku, Kyoto
* Entsu-ji: Iwakura Hataeda-cho, Sakyo-ku, Kyoto
   Fushimi Pavilion site: Momoyama Taichoro, Fushimi-ku, Kyoto
* Ginkaku-ji: Ginkakuji-cho, Sakyo-ku, Kyoto
   Heian Shrine: Okazaki Park, Nishi Tenno-cho, Sakyo-ku, Kyoto
   Hoshun-in: Daitoku-ji, Daitokuji-cho, Murasakino, Kita-ku, Kyoto
* Hyo-tei restaurant: Nanzenji Kusakawa-cho, Sakyo-ku, Kyoto
* Ishiyama-dera: Ishiyama Terabe-cho, Otsu, Shiga Prefecture
* Isui-en: 1–74 Suimon-cho, Nara City, Nara Prefecture
* Jiko-in: Koizumi-cho, Yamato Koriyama, Nara Prefecture
* Joju-in: Kiyomizu-dera, Kiyomizu 1-chome, Higashiyama-ku, Kyoto (private)
* Kamigamo Shrine: Kamigamo Yamamoto-cho, Kita-ku, Kyoto
* Kankyu-an teahouse: Mushanokoji Senke school of tea, Mushanokoji Ogawa, Kamikyo-ku, Kyoto (private)
* Kato residence: Shichijo Hommachi Higashi Iru, Higashiyama-ku, Kyoto (private)
* Kennin-ji: 4-chome, Yamato Oji Shijo Sagaru, Higashiyama-ku, Kyoto
   Kinkaku-ji: Kinugasa Kinkakuji-cho, Kita-ku, Kyoto
* Kitcho restaurant: Tenryu-ji, Saga, Ukyo-ku, Kyoto
* Kiyomizu residence: 67, 5-chome, Gojo Ohashi Higashi, Higashiyama-ku, Kyoto (private)
   Koto-in: Daitoku-ji, Daitokuji-cho, Murasakino, Kita-ku, Kyoto

* Kyoto Imperial Palace: Kyoto Imperial Garden, Sakai-machi, Maruta-cho, Kamikyo-ku, Kyoto (private; may be visited only with permission of Kyoto Office of Imperial Household Agency)
* Murin-an: Nanzenji Kusakawa-cho, Sakyo-ku, Kyoto (private; may be visited only with permission of Tourist Section, Kyoto Municipal Office)
  Myoshin-ji: Hanazono Myoshinji-cho, Ukyo-ku, Kyoto
  Nanshu-ji: Minami Hatago-cho, Sakai, Osaka Prefecture
* Ninna-ji: Omuro Ouchi, Ukyo-ku, Kyoto
  Obai-in: Daitoku-ji, Daitokuji-cho, Murasakino, Kita-ku, Kyoto
* Omote Senke school of tea: Ogawa Teranouchi Agaru, Kamikyo-ku, Kyoto (private)
* Onishi residence: Sanjo Kamaza, Nakakyo-ku, Kyoto (private)
* Raku residence: Aburakoji Nakadachiuri Agaru, Kamikyo-ku, Kyoto (private)
  Rokujo Kawara-in site: Rokujo, Kawara-machi, Shimogyo-ku, Kyoto
  Ryoan-ji: Ryoanji Goryonoshita-cho, Ukyo-ku, Kyoto
* Ryosoku-in: Kennin-ji, 4-chome, Yamato Oji Shijo Sagaru, Higashiyama-ku, Kyoto
* Shibata residence: Manjuji Miyuki-cho Sagaru, Shimogyo-ku, Kyoto (private)
  Shinju-an: Daitoku-ji, Daitokuji-cho, Murasakino, Kita-ku, Kyoto (private)
* Shinshin-an: Nanzenji Kusakawa-cho, Sakyo-ku, Kyoto (private)
* Shoden-ji: Nishigamo, Kita-ku, Kyoto
* Shoka-do: Iwashimizu Hachiman Shrine, Yawata-machi, Tsuzuki-gun, Kyoto Prefecture
* Shugaku-in villa: Shugaku-in, Sakyo-ku, Kyoto (private; may be visited only with permission of Kyoto Office of Imperial Household Agency)
* Sumiya: Shimabara Ageya-cho, Shimogyo-ku, Kyoto
* Suppon Dai-ichi restaurant: Shimo Choja-machi Sembon Nishi Iru, Kamikyo-ku, Kyoto
* Tabata residence: Ogawa Ebisugawa Agaru, Nakakyo-ku, Kyoto (private)
* Takeka inn, Tominaga-cho, Gion-machi, Higashiyama-ku, Kyoto
  Tawaraya confectionery: Muromachi Kamidachiuri Sagaru, Kamikyo-ku, Kyoto
* Tennenzue-tei: Otsu, Shiga Prefecture
* Tenryu-ji: Saga Susukinobaba, Ukyo-ku, Kyoto
  Toba Palace site: near Toba-jo Nangu, Minami-ku, Kyoto
* Uno residence: 6-chome, Gojozaka, Higashiyama-ku, Kyoto (private)
* Ura Senke school of tea: Ogawa Teranouchi Agaru, Kamikyo-ku, Kyoto (private)
* Warajiya restaurant: Shichijo Yamato Oji Nishi Iru, Higashiyama-ku, Kyoto
* Yabunouchi school of tea: Nishi no Toin Sagaru, Shimogyo-ku, Kyoto (private)

* Yamato Bunkakan: 969 Sugawara-cho, Nara City, Nara Prefecture
* Yanagi-jaya restaurant: Nara Park, Nara City, Nara Prefecture
  Yasuda residence: 1–80, Uzumasa San'o, Ukyo-ku, Kyoto (private)
* Yoda residence: 53, Shimogamo Izumi-cho, Sakyo-ku, Kyoto (private)
* Zenta residence: Anekoji Karasumaru Higashi Iru, Nakakyo-ku, Kyoto (private)

The "weathermark" identifies this book as having been planned, designed, and produced at the Tokyo offices of John Weatherhill, Inc., in collaboration with Tankosha. Book design and typography by Dana Levy. Layout of plates by Dana Levy and Nobu Miyazaki. Composed and printed by Kenkyusha Printing Company, Tokyo. Color and gravure plates engraved and printed by Nissha, Kyoto. Bound at the Makoto Binderies, Tokyo. The text is set in 12-point Monotype Bembo, with hand-set Bernhard Modern for display.